Developments in History Teaching

The Changing Classroom

General Editor: John Eggleston

Developments
in
History Teaching

Ian Steele

Open Books
London

First published 1976 by Open Books Publishing Ltd,
87–89 Shaftesbury Avenue, LONDON W1V 7AD

© Ian Steele 1976

Hardback: ISBN 0 7291 0046 4

Paperback: ISBN 0 7291 0041 3

Text set in 11/12 pt Photon Imprint, printed by photolithography, and bound in Great Britain at The Pitman Press, Bath

Contents

Editor's introduction

The theme of this series of books is the changing classroom. Everyone knows that schools change – that despite all the influences of tradition things aren't the same as they used to be. Yet during the past decade the change has been on such an unprecedented scale that in many ways schools have become surprising places not only to those who work with them – like parents and employers – but even to those who work in them, like teachers and students.

There are many reasons for these changes. Some are organisational, like the move to comprehensive secondary schooling, the raising of the school-leaving age, new pre-school classes, and 'destreaming', where children of all abilities work together. But even more spring from the way the teacher works in the classroom – from the increasing emphasis on individual methods, on creativity rather than remembering, on new patterns of assessment and examination, and on the use of a wide variety of project methods.

Such changes have certainly transformed the life of many classrooms and made school a different place for teachers and their students. This series is about life in those classrooms, for it is here that we can not only see change but understand it and get to grips with its effects on young people and on the society in which they will live.

In this volume Ian Steele writes about new developments in the teaching of history. What are the new methods of presentation that 'bring history to life' in the schools? What is the contribution being

made by the teaching of contemporary history to students' understanding of present-day society? Why is history usually an important component of integrated studies programmes in the schools? To
what extent are 'resources' augmenting the traditional history textbook? Ian Steele, a historian with extensive teaching experience,
analyses the new role of history in the curriculum, illustrates his
arguments from current practice, and reviews the developing future
of the subject.

John Eggleston

Acknowledgements

The author is grateful to the teachers and lecturers who have con-
tributed to Part II of this book, and to the headmasters of Clanfield
County Primary School, Hampshire; Clough Hall Comprehensive
School, Kidsgrove; Graham Balfour High School, Stafford; Priory
School for Boys, Shrewsbury; and the Sidney Stringer School and
Community College, Coventry, for permission to use activities in
their schools as the basis for the case studies.

PART I

1 History in danger — myth or reality?

The volume of criticism of history teaching today is considerable, and much of that criticism is undoubtedly justified. This does not mean, however, that the subject is faced with extinction. It reflects much more the appreciation of the fact that history has an important contribution to make in the education of schoolchildren, and indicates concern that the subject should be taught more effectively so that children might gain the maximum benefit from its study.

The teaching of history was subject to criticism in the nineteenth century in much the same way that it is today, and many of the comments made have a familiar ring to them. As early as 1807 Baldwin commented:

Too long have books designed for the instruction of children been written in a dry and repulsive style, which the pace and perseverance of our maturer years would scarcely enable us to conquer. Too long have their tender memories been loaded with a variety of minute particulars which, as they excite no passion in the mind, and present no picture, can be learned only to forget.

The H.M.I. for Ipswich and Edmonton in 1879 commented that elementary school teachers acted wisely in leaving the subject alone, noting in his report (Danby 1880):

The course of historical teaching is too extensive, and its arrangement . . . is ill adapted to the capabilities and wants of children in public elementary schools. In fact a scholar painfully struggling to learn the history of England from an unnamed epoch before the Norman Conquest to the death of George III, too often only commits to memory lists of dates and strings of names; these are soon forgotten and leave behind them no knowledge at all of the growth of the English nation.

Distinguished academics were also highly critical. In the same year Freeman (1879), later to become Regius Professor of History in Oxford, told the Liverpool Institute that history teaching was deficient because it consisted largely in 'loading the child's memory without ever appealing to the imagination. He is overwhelmed with words and names, without being taught to attach any ideas to the words and names.' As a result those who could think for themselves lived through the process, learning 'not so much through their teaching, as in spite of their teaching', while the others perished intellectually.

The comments made on history teaching today, by both academics and teachers, are frequently similar in character to those made in the earlier period. Fines (1969) has complained that children have been bored to tears by syllabuses geared to the memorisation of facts, and in this context he noted:

Above all the same nonsensical methods decried years ago continue in the schools: notes are dictated, passages learned off by heart, vast periods are scampered over so quickly that no real understanding can possibly be achieved, and the fetish of chronological sequence holds sway in spite of everything that has been said against it.

Similarly Barker (1974), a teacher in the Sir Frederick Osborne School, Welwyn Garden City, commented sarcastically that:

Despite the colours and sounds of modern publishing and audio visual aids, history is probably the least changed of school subjects. It is very rare to see desks in anything but rows. A short lecture supported by a question and answer routine and written work is the staple teaching method.

Such depressing descriptions are to some extent deceptive. Striking progress has been made for example in the production of resources for history teaching — archive and project kits, resource and topic books, slide sets, etc. — and the problem for the teacher is more one of selection than availability. Similarly the development of radio, television, film and tape has opened up new dimensions in history teaching. Changes have also taken place in the interpretation of history and its role in schools. Considerable progress has been made in the understanding of children's thinking and how this is relevant to history in the classroom. It must be acknowledged, however, that the above developments have significantly influenced activities in only a minority of classrooms, hence the general criticism of history teaching. If the subject is to maintain its position in the curriculum it is evident that the advances already made must be implemented on a much wider scale. Whether this happens will depend very much on the individual teacher, who holds the key to what actually happens in the classroom.

At the present time the teacher's plight is an unenviable one as he is subject to many pressures. There is considerable evidence that, while history 'languishes' in schools, it is flourishing as never before with the adult population. In 1972 a lecturer at the London University Institute noted, for example, that 'as a leisure pursuit history is a growth industry, enjoyed not for the philosophically weak reason that it helps to explain the present, but because it exists in its own right, establishing exhilarating contrasts with the present, nourishing both intellect and imagination' (Bryant 1972). Certainly adult local history courses are flourishing, the attendance at buildings and monuments of historical interest is increasing, and television programmes on historical characters, be they monarchs or explorers, draw large viewing audiences. The history teacher has to reconcile these facts with the considerable volume of evidence suggesting that history is unpopular in school. The findings of the Schools Council Enquiry 1 (1968) which investigated the attitude of school-leavers towards a range of subjects has caused much embarrassment to history teachers. It revealed for instance that the pupils surveyed regarded history as one of the most useless and boring of subjects. Reasons quoted for this included repetition, lack of understanding and failure to achieve success in the subject. Typical comments on the way in which the subject was taught were: 'They went on and on, the same thing over and over again', and 'It's the way we are getting it, no discussions, just questions. We have to look up the answers.' Similarly Blishen (1969) quoted Judith (age fourteen) to the effect that: 'I awake to a sickening thud each Monday morning – double History, eighty minutes of the toneless drone of the master's voice and the pendulum swing of his leg over the desk.'

Faced by evidence such as this, the history teacher – and it should be remembered that in many instances, particularly in primary schools, he is not a trained historian – is placed in a very difficult position. He can only counter the criticism that history is 'useless' by showing how it can make a distinctive contribution to the education of children. Unfortunately for the teacher even the professional historians seem to have difficulty in reaching agreement on the nature of their subject. On the one hand there are the traditional historians, championed by Elton (1967), who pursue very much a separatist line for history. On the other hand there is the 'progressive' school, which is characterised by an anxiety both to make history more 'relevant' and by its intention to develop a closer relationship between history and associated disciplines. Lack of agreement about the nature of history in academic circles does not make for confidence in its integrity as a school subject, particularly when the claims of new disciplines about which there is agreement, such as politics and sociology, are being pushed forward vigorously.

The history teacher has problems to face other than justifying his subject. In common with his colleagues he is likely to have a full timetable, with all the associated preparation and marking, and therefore time for reading history for its own sake or keeping pace with developments in pedagogical techniques is very limited. Even if he can keep track of the growing list of resources, lack of finance will restrict his choice. If he wishes to innovate and introduce, for example, a greater element of field work, there is likely to be considerable resistance in school because of the implications of blocked lessons for the timetable. Even within the subject he faces major difficulties. He may read, for example, articles on history teaching such as that by Collister (1972) in which he is informed that the pupils

need to know the highlights of the national heritage and how their own particular locality can reflect great events . . . Our pupils must know something
of the great giants of the modern world – the U.S.A., Russia and China, and
how history has shaped them, they must know something of great crises and
heroic ages.

At the same time the history teacher is expected to develop objectivity and powers of criticism in his pupils. It is anticipated that he will
pass on the cultural heritage and also instil a sense of morality and
humanity. The pupils are expected to acquire a pride in their nation's
past, but at the same time an awareness of the wider world. In addition the pupils' historical imaginations are to be stimulated so that
they can project themselves back into the past. In view of the fact
that the majority of secondary school children terminate their
historical studies at the end of the third year, it would seem that a
great deal is being asked of the history teacher and that one source of
his weakness is that he is expected to do too much. Certainly his load
is heavier than that of teachers of any other subject, and he could be
forgiven for looking enviously at other areas, for example
mathematics, modern languages and science, where the time allocation is greater and the role much more clearly defined.

It is hardly surprising that, as Rogers (1967) noted, the history
teacher does not seem very interested in improving himself. He is
concerned with his image in the school – with pupils, fellow staff,
headmaster and parents – and examination results play a large part
in establishing that image. Thus he is unlikely to face squarely the
wider issues that confront history teaching today. The history
teacher is also very much the prisoner of his own educational
background and the numerous constraints that have been described
above. Yet we cannot escape the fact that, if there is to be an advance
in history teaching, it has to take place in the classroom, and ultimately the attitude and knowledge of the individual teacher hold
the key to the future.

It is the intention in the first part of this book to examine the basic
problems facing history teachers today and show what progress is
being made in overcoming them. Thus attention will be paid to
thinking on the nature of the subject and to establishing whether it

can make a distinctive contribution to the school curriculum. The place of aims and objectives in history teaching will be analysed, and the role of evaluation – with particular reference to external examinations. Developments in the understanding of child psychology and the associated implications for teaching strategy will also be investigated. Through the exploration of these themes it is anticipated that the history teacher will be able to inform himself on the state of his subject in schools and so become more effective in teaching it.

Conclusion

History is not in danger as a school subject, although the days of the traditional approach to its teaching may well be numbered. Contemporary society has shown itself to be very interested in its past and it is inevitable that this interest will be reflected in the school curriculum. What is required, however, is a much greater awareness of the basic problems facing history teachers, and sufficient material has been produced on these, which, if it were widely known, could revolutionise the teaching of the subject. It is the responsibility of the history teacher to acquaint himself with developments in his subject and to employ his findings in the classroom. It is hoped that the contents of this book will provide him with some assistance towards the achievement of this massive, but very important task.

2 Changes in the discipline of history and its place in the school curriculum

As the instrument of society for the education of the young, the curriculum will reflect the ideals, knowledges and skills that are believed to be significant, or that are related to the common activities of the members of that society. (Smith, Stanley and Shores 1971)

The truth of this was demonstrated during the nineteenth century when the establishment of history as a separate discipline was paralleled by its acceptance as a subject in the school curriculum. Further, Bramwell (1973) has suggested that, of the factors determining the nature of the curriculum, the subject specialist force has 'most frequently been explicitly linked with curricular change', a point amplified by Connell-Smith and Lloyd (1974) when they noted how 'university approaches to the subject greatly influence the way history is taught elsewhere, and determine the materials at the disposal of its teachers'. During the nineteenth century university history was characterised by concentration on the outline of political and constitutional British history, the subject being taught, in the main, through mass lectures, and assessed through essay-based examinations. These features also became characteristic of school history and their legacy is still with us.

It follows that if developments in university history in the past played a part of shaping the school history curriculum, the same is likely to be true today. An appreciation of current developments in the universities is in fact necessary for an understanding of what is happening in schools. University history is quite evidently in a state of flux and far-reaching changes are taking place. The most noticeable developments are in the areas of study, and the emphasis on contemporary and world history has been particularly marked. In 1971, for example, the great majority of universities taught English and European history beyond 1939 while nearly all offered courses in American history and almost half in African history (Blows 1971). Rather surprisingly, however, other areas which have received a great deal of publicity are still not very well established, local, urban and scientific history being good examples. In 1971 less than a quarter of the universities ran local history courses, and very few taught urban history. Science history was similarly neglected, and Gowling (1975) complained in her inaugural lecture in Oxford of the precarious footing of the subject, commenting that its omission resulted in 'intellectual improverishment for the students and historical impoverishment for the profession'.

The most surprising area of neglect in university courses, however, is in the methodology of history. The demand for the methodological training of students is a longstanding one. As early as 1788 Priestley made a plea for its inclusion in history courses. Firth (1904) commented in his inaugural lecture that: 'This lecture is a plea for giving future historians a proper professional training in Oxford, and therefore an attack on the system of historical training which renders it impossible.' The training he had in mind was that provided in French and German universities: 'a training in the methods of investigation, in the use of original authorities, and in those auxiliary sciences which the Germans call "Hilfswissenschaften".' The lack of recognition of the value of a training of this type by colleges was described by Firth as 'a notorious fact' and he complained that: 'Nearly all of us who teach history in Oxford have received no training of this kind.' Seventy years later there are still alarming gaps. In 1971, for example, only sixteen of the forty universities offered special courses in historical method or historiography and in only six of these were they compulsory (Blows 1971). Where such courses are established the pattern varies, but these do tend to be found in the newer universities. The students at the Open University, for example, study history methodology as part of the foundation integrated humanities course. Similarly students at the School of English and American Studies in East Anglia are introduced to history method in the first two terms, whereas at York students do not study history method, historiography and the relationship of history to other disciplines until the end of the second year.

It would be misleading to exaggerate the extent of change in the areas studied in British universities. Much that is traditional still has a very firm footing. In 1971 over three-quarters of the universities ran courses in medieval English and European history, and in the majority of these the medieval English history course was compulsory. A substantial majority of the universities ran courses that provided scope for the continuous study of British history and in most cases such courses were compulsory. Nevertheless it should be noted that even in the traditional areas the character of the courses was quite likely to be changing, contemporary interests being reflected in the study of the medieval period if there was focus on 'radicalism, social class, technology and economics, rather than on religion, political theory, agricultural history and diplomacy ...' (Harrison 1968).

A factor further complicating the position of history in the universities is the increasing tendency to study it alongside other disciplines. Although history may still be studied as a single subject, this is now becoming the exception rather than the rule. Milne (1974), for example, has noted that: 'The single degree syllabus ... is now regarded paradoxically as suitable only for those aiming at historical research for a higher degree.' The building of closer links between disciplines has led also to some fundamental organisational changes within universities, the most striking being, in some instances, the elimination of the separate history faculty. At the University of Kent, for example, historians are to be found in the Faculties of Humanities and Social Studies, whereas at Sussex University they are located in the five 'Schools' of English and American Studies, European Studies, Social Sciences, African and Asian Studies, and Cultural and Community Studies.

Just as the historical areas of study in the universities are changing, so too – although progress is very slow – are the ways in which they are approached. The outline syllabus still plays an important part in university courses; Bush (1973), for example, a lecturer at Manchester University, complained:

No matter what the changes of the last decade in the content, teaching and examination of university courses in history, the traditional system of providing students with preliminary outline courses in preparation for final optional and special optional subjects continues to dominate the typical syllabus.

Even the methods of teaching and forms of assessment have not undergone any substantial change as yet. The compulsory mass lecture is slowly giving ground to optional lectures, while the use of seminars and tutorials is increasing, but the standard assessment procedure remains the essay-based examination. It is significant that in 1971 only twenty-six of the forty universities made provision for the students to write a thesis, and that such a thesis was compulsory in only seven (Blows 1971). The writing of a thesis is the closest the history student can come to working in the style of the professional historian and one would anticipate that such work would loom large in assessment procedures. Yet the evidence suggests that work of this kind is still low on the list of priorities of a substantial number of university history departments.

The Schools Council Paper, *Humanities for the Young School Leaver: An Approach Through History* (1969), commented that 'history teachers in an educational system evolving new structures and new styles to meet the demands of a rapidly changing society cannot escape the obligation to face and accept new approaches to the syllabus and to teaching methods.' It follows that, if this is the case, the history teacher must look closely at the debate on the relationship between history and other disciplines, and at the growth of relatively new areas of study – world and contemporary history, demography, etc. The changes taking place in universities are already reflected, to some extent, in schools. Within the last decade, for example, there has been a noticeable increase in schools in the teaching of world, contemporary and local history. Similarly there has been a tendency to study history alongside other subjects in integrated or social studies courses. In some cases departments have been regrouped with history becoming part of a humanities department. Further, there is evidence of change in C.S.E., O and A level examinations in that the essay is tending to occupy a less significant place than in the past while there has been a corresponding increase in emphasis in projects or special studies. The changes taking place, however, should not be allowed to obscure the basic need. The teacher must seek to identify the nature of history and thereby establish whether it can make a distinctive contribution to the education of children. If he can do this he will be better placed to face and accept new approaches to the syllabus and teaching methods.

History is quite different from the other social sciences. Trevelyan described it as the house in which all other subjects dwell. Equally, because it calls on other disciplines to aid its investigations, it does have much that is interdisciplinary in its character. Its individuality has been well brought out by Luthy (1968) when he noted that, in contrast to most systematic sciences, history

does not aim initially at generalization and theoretical formalization. Instead it aims at individualization, identification, at working out the singular qualities of all human events which, although they always reveal certain similarities with other human events of a related type and hence form part of the sum of human experience, are never exactly repeated with the same background and under the same conditions; nor are they susceptible to experimental repetition.

It is in fact the establishment of the unique that is the specific aim of historical study, and current developments in the universities should not be allowed to obscure that basic point. Thus the increased use of the concepts and generalisations of the social sciences has to be seen as part of the process of improving the understanding and communication of the uniqueness of whichever aspect of the human past is being studied. Similarly the movement towards new areas of study in university history – world, contemporary, demographic, local, etc. – should not disguise the fact that the essence of the discipline remains the same, no matter which area is being studied. For each pupil the study of history is an individual exercise, and if he understands the nature of what he is trying to do the area of study is almost irrelevant. It is likely, for instance, that the fifth-form pupil in a grammar school will find the study of the Children's Crusade just as relevant and meaningful as an examination of the historical background to the Arab–Israeli conflict or to the unrest in Northern Ireland. In each case the pupil's intention should be, at his own level, to establish that which is distinctive and unique in the area being studied, and it is this which gives the discipline unity.

A second unifying factor which is becoming increasingly important in the universities, and with which the teacher in school must come to terms, is the methodology of the subject. The universities themselves have neglected this area in the past, but the pressures for its development are mounting. In this context Hurstfield (1968) of University College, London, has commented:

I have often told my students, undergraduate or postgraduate, that I do not care whether they accept my conclusions but I do deeply care that they should learn something from my methods. The methods of history are severe and exacting. They involve the search for new sources; the critical re-examination of old ones; the assembly and testing of evidence; the inquiry into new methods of social investigation; the application of reason to establish a pattern of causes, economic, political, cultural, in man's relations with a changing society.

It is evident that the methodology of history has been neglected in schools in the past. Hurstfield (1969) himself has complained that, in too many cases, the student has not got beyond the 'pedestrian narrative'. Similarly Russell (1968) of Bedford College has bewailed the fact that 'Most first-year undergraduates are at their most uncomfortable when faced with the controversies between historians', implying that, because of their school training, the undergraduates' capacity to think for themselves was underdeveloped. The development of the skills necessary for the study of history can only be part of a long-term and carefully planned process and it therefore follows that a training in the methods of historical study should be built into the syllabus from the very beginnings of the pupil's introduction to history.

Conclusion

Much of the criticism of history teaching in schools today is undoubtedly justified and it is difficult to disagree with the comment of Beevers (1969) that: 'Those who teach in schools find the typical history syllabus derided as remote from their pupils' interests and irrelevant to their needs, except for the purposes of examinations.' If teachers can take account of developments in history at a university level they will be in a better position to stifle much of that criticism. In particular they will have to be able to identify the distinctive characteristics of history and communicate them to their pupils. They must also be aware of the possible contributions of the new areas of study – local history and demography, world and contemporary history, etc. – to the enrichment of the pupils' learning, while at the same time changing the emphasis from the content to the process of study. It must not be overlooked, however, that many other factors will also affect the teaching of history; prominent among these will be advances in child psychology and in curriculum theory, particularly in the framing and assessment of aims and objectives and the related developments in teaching techniques and resources.

3 Psychology and history teaching

The development of the child's capacity to think is only partly the product of physical maturation. It is also greatly affected by his learning experiences, both inside and outside the school situation. The psychologist, in trying to explain how the child's thought processes develop, is in a position of fundamental importance as he can contribute a great deal to the history teacher's understanding of what is happening in the classroom. He may, for example, throw light on what motivates children, explain how concepts are formed and logical thought develops, show how and when children acquire a sense of time, and focus attention on the importance of language in the history lesson. Yet is must not be overlooked that it is the history teacher's responsibility to plan and organise his own courses and that he should use the results of the psychologist's research as and when it seems appropriate.

THE DEVELOPMENT OF CHILDREN'S THINKING
In recent years much attention has been paid to the idea that children pass through various stages as their thought processes develop. The most influential contribution in this field has been made by Piaget working in Geneva; his findings have provided the basis for much of the research done in this country. Piaget has suggested that there are three basic stages in the development of the thinking of the child: the pre-operational, the concrete operational, and the formal operational, and that these levels are interdependent, one level having to be consolidated before the next can be reached.

The acceptance of the idea that the child passes through these different stages as his thinking develops leads to important questions for the history teacher. To what extent can the development of historical thinking be related to the stages described by Piaget? If a child does pass through these stages, does the transition take place at the same age as may be expected in other subjects, such as science? Is it possible, or even desirable, to accelerate the process of transition? How can a teacher assess the level a child has reached? What methods and materials are appropriate to the different levels? The problems are extremely complex and added complications exist for the teacher because, within a class, there is likely to be considerable variation in the thinking levels of its members. The psychologists, however, have produced sufficient material to provide answers to some of the questions listed above.

The research carried out suggests that the Piagetian stages do apply to the development of historical understanding, although the ages at which the transition from one stage to another takes place tends to be later than in other subjects. The most prolific writer in this area has been Hallam (1967) whose initial research was carried out in a Bradford school. Hallam tested 100 children, twenty from each year in a secondary school; he found that they were reaching the concrete operational level of thought in their twelfth year, and a formal operational level at the age of 16.2–16.6 years. Hallam quoted examples of concrete and formal operational thought on the part of his subjects who, for example, having read a passage on William I, were asked whether they thought William was cruel. One pupil, aged 15.10 years and with an I.Q. of 110 answered:

'I think he was cruel because he laid waste to the land but he allowed the people to collect the bodies of the people they wanted to bury.'
'What does this prove then?'
'He could be cruel in winning a battle, but after the battle was over he could allow the people more scope.'

This answer was judged to be at a concrete operational level because, while being closely linked to the material in the extract, it failed to coordinate the different facts. In contrast a 14.8-year-old pupil with an I.Q. of 127 answered at a formal operational level:

'It depends what you call cruel. If the definition of cruel is to kill and ravish and burn for any purpose whatever, William was cruel. On the other hand if one is prepared to accept political necessity, William's cruelty was justified . . .'

The extracts illustrate beautifully the different levels of thought, and Hallam's findings have been largely supported, with slight modifications, by other psychologists. Stones (1965) working with secondary school children in Birmingham found that their thinking was largely concrete and descriptive during the first three years of their school careers, but in the fourth and fifth their answers showed an increasing capacity to engage in abstract thought. More recently De Silva (1972) has carried out a highly sophisticated research project with a cross-section of the ability range of 160 children aged eleven to sixteen in a Birmingham comprehensive school. His work indicates that the turning point in the transition from descriptive to explanatory modes of thought is in the age range thirteen to fourteen. It is evident that children develop the capacity to think in the abstract rather later in history than in other areas of the curriculum, and it is likely that many children leave school still operating at a concrete operational level.

It has not been clearly established that one can accelerate the transition from one level of thought to another, but there is evidence that the teacher can improve the quality of the thought processes. Two Canadians, Bate and Moore (1975), have looked into the development of historical thinking. Their research, based on Calgary high schools, indicated that an experimental group of fifteen-year-old students made substantially faster progress than the control group in developing their critical thinking ability in the year that followed their pursuing a course in the basic processes of historical thought. Many questions will have to be answered before it can be established that a formal training in historical method does have a long-term effect on the pupil's thinking. None the less, it is quite evident that the different levels of thought do need specialised attention and one area to which the teacher must pay particular regard is the use of language in developing historical thinking.

THE PLACE OF LANGUAGE IN HISTORY TEACHING

Increasing notice is being taken of the relationship between the development of language and the growth of thinking skills and at the present time this is one of the most important, but also most difficult problems facing the history teacher. It is particularly complex in history because most of the vocabulary in common use in the history classroom is of an abstract nature while the great majority of children in secondary schools are thinking at a concrete operational level and depend largely on their immediate experience for understanding.

There is a great deal of evidence that children are unable to digest much of their historical diet. Charlton (1952) analysed the understanding of a group of fourteen-year-olds of thirty key words used in their textbooks. He found that, although over fourth-fifths of the pupils thought they understood the words – which covered economic, political and religious concepts – less than half of the words were in fact understood, and that even the best pupils did not comprehend more than twenty. Similarly Coltham (1960) investigated the understanding of a group of top juniors, with a mental age ranging from eight to sixteen, of the terms 'king, early man, invasion, ruler, trade, and subject', and she also found a wide range in the levels of understanding. More specifically Hannam (1968) has quoted a striking example of misunderstanding on the part of the pupil who thought Wolsey wanted to shoot the Pope because he read that 'Wolsey aimed at the Papacy'. Bernbaum (1972) has pointed out the likely confusion which might arise in a description of Henry VIII confiscating monastic 'lands': to the historian the term implies a great source of wealth and an area of patronage whereas to the pupil it may imply simply fields. Such examples clearly provide the history teacher with food for thought!

The problems of understanding historical vocabulary can arise in several ways. It may be that completely new terms are being introduced to the pupils. If this is the case a teacher dealing with such terms as 'democracy', 'Renaissance' or 'Reformation' is likely to try to explain them. This in itself is a skilled process and will be looked at more closely in a later section when the psychologists' suggestions on how improvements may be effected are considered. Just as complex as the problem of defining new words, however, is the difficulty in establishing the accuracy of the pupil's understanding of words with which he is already familiar. Children often think they understand a word because they have seen or read it in the past. Alternatively they may have learned the definition of a word without really understanding it. Peel (1967) has focused attention on these difficulties, noting that some words, such as church and law, already 'carry existing personal and concrete meanings', and that the child will tend to carry these over erroneously. There are many such words which the teacher is likely to assume the children understand and will not therefore try to explain. Take, as a simple example, the word 'factory'. The pupils in a class will already have varying concepts of a twentieth-century factory which are likely to be carried over when the word is used in an eighteenth-century context. The scope for misunderstanding is clear and is undoubtedly a source of weakness.

The efficient use of language is fundamental to good history teaching. It might be called, as Coltham (1971) has noted, 'the enabling factor in education' and it is certainly true that the use of language is critical in concept formation and the movement towards the higher levels of thinking. Clearly particular levels of thinking are closely interwoven with the stage reached in language development, and, if history teaching is to improve, much more attention will have to be paid to the relationship between the two.

THE CHILD'S UNDERSTANDING OF TIME

Traditionally the history teacher has been very concerned with the concept of time. The chronological-outline syllabus was intended to establish a framework of time within which historical events could be located, and the associated memorisation of dates has been a characteristic feature of history lessons for a great many of our pupils. Research on the child's understanding of time has been limited. It has concentrated more on time in general than on historical time and on what is understood rather than on what might be understood. It has shown however that many assumptions about the child's capacity to understand time have been in error.

Jahoda (1963) collated much of the research that had then been carried out on the child's understanding of time. He noted the confusion, at the age of five, of time and space and pointed out that time was not 'a uniform and homogeneous flow, but tied to particular objects, locations or events'. It is around the age of five that the child does begin to order past events into earlier or later, though understanding at this stage is still very simple and even 'yesterday' and 'tomorrow' can cause difficulty. Certainly 'last week' means very little, 'last year' even less and 'the nineteenth century' has no meaning whatsoever for the young pupil. According to Jahoda the ability to name the year when something happened – several independent investigators agree that the child can do this at about the age of eight – does not mean that the child can understand the broader chronological system. Work carried out by Oakden and Sturt (1922) and Bradley (1947) suggested that it was not until the age of eleven that children understood the basic implications of historical dates. There seems to be general support, among psychologists who have worked in the area, that the age of eleven does mark the turning point in the child's understanding of time. Flickinger and Rehage (1949) came to the conclusion that the child gains some concept of the past at the age of eight, a full understanding of our system of reckoning time at about eleven, an understanding of time lines at about thirteen, and maturity of understanding of time words and dates at about sixteen. Research carried out by Friedman in 1944 further supports this estimate of the rate of development (Wallace 1965). Where results have been published that vary from the pattern described above, they suggest that the child's understanding of time develops even more slowly. Rogers (1967), for example, tried to differentiate the concept of time in general from that of historical time and found a marked improvement in the overall concept of time between the ages of 13.6 and 14.6, but a much slower improvement in the understanding of historical time.

Efforts have also been made to see if it is possible to improve children's concepts relating to historical time. Pistor worked with an experimental and a control group covering the age range nine to eleven and found that there were no significant differences between the groups, thus suggesting that the child's increase in understanding of historical time is 'more a function of mental maturation, coupled with the widening of general experience, than of purely formal teaching' (Hallam 1970). The research carried out by Vikainen in Finland with slightly older children found rather differently and the performance of the experimental group was slightly superior, not only in the understanding of historical time, but in other aspects of history too (Wallace 1965). It may well be that the two sets of results are not as contradictory as they appear at first glance. Understanding of historical time is highly likely to be a product of mental maturation, but equally, once a particular stage has been reached, it may be possible to accelerate the development of that understanding.

The implications of psychological research for history in the classroom

Psychologists have exposed numerous weaknesses in the history classroom. They have illustrated the futility of attempting to teach history as an abstract subject to minds working at a stage well below the formal operational level. They have shown the importance of the careful use of language in developing understanding and have questioned the assumption that children can understand the chronological framework on which many history syllabuses are based. In addition to asking questions, however, they have also tried to provide some answers, and much that is worthwhile has emerged. Underlying all is the need for the teacher to be able to identify the level of his pupils' thinking so that he can use it as a foundation for encouraging mental growth.

LANGUAGE AND UNDERSTANDING
A vital question is whether the child's grasp of historical terms, whether he is thinking at a concrete or a formal operational level, can be improved so that his thought processes are more effective. Both Coltham and Bernbaum recommend that much closer attention be paid to historical vocabulary. Recognising the crucial importance of taking the children's previous experience into account in developing understanding Coltham (1971) suggests that it is

certainly worthwhile for teachers when selecting any materials or topics for study, to consider listing the particular terms which will be required and judging whether or not special attention to their meaning will still be necessary at some stage – or even to decide that, given the previous experience of *this* group of children, another topic would be more desirable.

She recognises that vocabulary lessons at the beginning of the study of a new topic might be rather dull, but points out that a quick check of the understanding of basic terms might be achieved through the use of duplicated sheets showing varying definitions of terms and requiring children to tick the one they think appropriate. Some justification for the use of a 'programmed' approach has been found in the research of Stones (1967) at Manchester University in which she found the ability of adolescents to think in historical terms was significantly improved after they had studied a unit teaching the definitions and the interrelationship of important concepts used in her material.

Bernbaum (1972) recommends that history teachers should look for the words in common use that may need to be defined more precisely, as well as the longer and more complex terms that will more obviously need explanation. He further suggests that words of a high level of abstraction should be avoided where possible, although sometimes they must be used. Particular criticism is made of headings such as 'political causes' and 'economic causes', as these do not communicate a great deal to the pupil. Where words of a high level of abstraction have to be used it is recommended that the pupil works up to, rather than down from them. In studying the Industrial Revolution, for instance, Bernbaum questions the value of working down from the headings 'transport, power, social distress', and recommends working up from subheadings of a lower level of abstraction, for example, 'roads, canals, steam engines, lack of food, shortage of work'. In this way it is anticipated that pupils will develop their linguistic skills and also their capacity to analyse and communicate their ideas on the subject being studied.

The fundamental point is that the great majority of pupils in secondary schools up to the age of sixteen are still thinking at a concrete operational level and thus, if they are to understand a new term, r a variation in the definition of a term with which they are already familiar, they must be able to relate it directly to their own experience. It follows that the history they study should not be over-abstract in form and consequently lecturing must be viewed with great suspicion as it conceals children's lack of understanding. Hallam (1970) has advocated the use of discussion, particularly in small groups of four or five, but he acknowledges that it is not yet proved that such activities, although more enjoyable, do lead to a development in thinking skills. Hallam also suggests that thinking ability will be developed if children are asked to hold and balance facts or views that seem to contrast. Thus with children who think at a pre-operational level, and who are progressing towards concrete operational level, the teacher should indicate two aspects of a historical character or situation in order to bring in the force of equilibration. Similarly progress towards the formal operational level might be speeded up by the teacher having a policy of presenting at least four points of view on any historical topic. Further, in setting written work, the teacher should give exercises demanding inter-pretation and reflection as it is anticipated that these will stimulate the development of thinking skills. Examples of exercises of this type suggested are asking the pupil to project himself into another time, recreating dialogues between people of opposing views, finding causal links and relationships, and requiring the pupil to contrast his own life with the life of others in the past.

It also follows that if pupils are thinking at a pre-operational or concrete operational level there must be a heavy concentration on the use of teaching aids. The range of aids available today is vast – film strips, slides, pictures, maps, diagrams, tapes, films, textbooks, archive teaching units, games, simulation exercises, etc. Their usefulness is closely related to the pupil's ability to understand them. Thus they may be seen as a means of increasing the pupil's interest in the subject, but they must also be viewed as a means of developing the pupil's language skills and hence improving his historical un-derstanding. The relationship between the two is obviously very close, but the second aspect is vital yet frequently neglected. Although there are many audio-visual aids available they are rarely used in some classrooms so that, inevitably, much of what transpires in the history lesson takes place at a high level of abstraction and is therefore counterproductive.

One further aspect of the teaching of linguistic skills that must be explored was well brought out by Honeybone (1971) in his interesting article on 'The development of formal historical thought in schoolchildren'. Using the research findings of De Silva (1969), he notes that success in history at school demands a high verbal I.Q. and that conversely children with a low verbal I.Q. are less likely to be successful. Consequently, if courses continue to be based on conceptual verbalisation, they will remain unattractive to all but the literate and verbal élite. Honeybone's conclusion is therefore that, if history is to remain as a valid school subject, there must be less emphasis on abstraction. Thus a greater variety of methods should be employed and the use of abilities other than verbal encouraged. Such an approach might seem to threaten the integrity of the subject, but this is not the case. The American psychologist Bruner (1960) made an important contribution to thinking in this area when he suggested that the real quarry was the mode of inquiry of the specialist so that, if the structure of the subject could be defined, any topic could be taught to any child at any age. Honeybone's argument was that the child should work in the style of the historian and should therefore encounter the type of evidence available to the historian. The difference between the two would be in their levels of perception and, because the pupil has fewer preconceptions, the level of his thought would be less advanced (Honeybone 1971). This view has much to recommend it and clearly relates closely to the psychologists' recommendations on what is appropriate for children thinking at a pre-operational or concrete operational level – the need for the use of activity methods, visual evidence, and so on.

Obviously some forms of evidence are of greater value than others. A great variety of documentary evidence is now available for use in schools and the proliferation of archive teaching units and 'Jackdaw'-type kits, for example, bears full testimony to what has been happening. Documents dealing with abstract and complex themes, such as religious or political tracts, are unlikely to be as effective as eye-witness descriptions of events such as the Black Hole of Calcutta, or the Massacre of Peterloo. The latter two examples would provide ample scope for the analyses of cause and effect, detection of bias, etc. Similarly visual aids, be they film strip, photograph, slide or three-dimensional model, can be subject to historical analysis. Historical evidence in the field is another greatly neglected source which could be used to develop historical skills in a systematic and interesting way. It may be a moot point whether or not it is possible to accelerate the transition from one level of thinking to another, but it would be very difficult to deny the possibility that the thinking of a child at any one stage could be made much more effective by a systematic training in the use of historical skills, and through a closer attention to the place of language in the development of understanding.

THE PLACE OF MOTIVATION

It goes without saying that unless the pupil is motivated little learning will take place. In Schools Council Enquiry 1 (1968) many pupils commented that they were bored by subjects they felt were useless to them. Typical of the general attitude was the comment of one student: 'I think we have too much of them. Most of these subjects we don't need and we don't take an interest in them. What's the use of knowing them if we don't need them?' Not a great deal has been written on the problems of motivation with particular reference to history, but a number of general points have been made which are obviously relevant.

Material has been published on the areas children find interesting in history, though some of this is contradictory. The modern trend, particularly with fourth and fifth forms, is to teach more modern history on the basis that the students will be more highly motivated because they see it as relevant. In contrast the research of Musgrove (1963) suggests that it is the distant past which has the greatest appeal to children and that this is true of all ages, including boys and girls aged ten to fifteen in grammar and secondary modern schools. Coltham (1971) has also commented on the interests of children and suggested that the younger ones are generally more interested in action, in the contrast between their own lives and other times and places, in drama and narrative. The older children, in contrast, are more attracted by analysing 'what makes people tick'; considering arguments for and against a given course of action, and studying the conditions that give rise to causes and movements. Such a comment brings us back to the stages of development in children's thinking, and it is worth making the rather obvious point that if the pupil is faced with a task which demands that he be active, which is within his competence but which offers a challenge to him, and which is concerned with the story of man in the past, the area being studied is likely to be of secondary importance.

STRATEGIES FOR DEVELOPING AN UNDERSTANDING OF TIME

The difficulties experienced by children in understanding historical time have already been commented on but this does not mean that the concept should be ignored. Psychologists have commented on techniques that might be employed to aid understanding and Jahoda (1963), for example, argued against the use of time charts with young children and advocated starting in the present and working back in order to develop a time perspective. Cohen (1954), in contrast, saw a useful place for dates and time charts, even with young children, although he too argued that, initially, there must be discussion of events within the child's realised time, and a start made in the present.

The most substantial contribution in this very neglected area has again been made by Coltham (1971) who has argued that, since the concept of time is abstract and cannot be acquired quickly, practice in using a time scheme should be spread over several years, the optimum period being when the concrete operational level of thought is well advanced. Thus, when pupils had encountered a range of events or personalities from several periods, and topics from varying parts of the world at both 'concurrent and separate' times, the point would have been reached when these could be organised on a temporal basis. She also makes the very important point that younger children are more concerned with collecting material that may be used later, but that it is more important for them to gain an imaginative grasp of the past than temporal relationships. A similar point should be made about children thinking at a concrete operational level of thought. While it is important that they should gain an understanding of temporal relationships, there are higher priorities, in particular ensuring that the pupils are favourably disposed towards the subject, and that they see its study as a worthwhile end in itself.

Conclusion

Although many areas remain to be explored, such as the role of history in developing a sense of nationalism and in preparing the ground for moral judgements, and much further research is also needed into the areas touched upon in this chapter, it is evident that the psychologists have already had a fundamental impact on the teaching of history in this country. They have thrown considerable light on the stages through which a child passes as his thinking skills develop, and have related this to the teaching of history. In particular they have focused attention on the basic importance of language in the development of historical understanding. They have made the history teacher question many of his assumptions, the most obvious being that the pupil has a meaningful grasp of the concept of time before the age of sixteen; this has important implications for the teaching of history in the classroom. It must again be stressed, however, that it is up to the history teacher to make his own decisions about what to teach, and how to teach it. The history teacher is concerned with the integrity of his subject whereas the psychologist is concerned with explaining how children's thinking develops. Consequently, it remains the history teacher's responsibility to use the findings of the psychologist so that he can teach his subject more effectively.

4 Aims and objectives in history teaching

The character of aims and objectives

The past decade has seen a proliferation in colleges and universities of courses in curriculum theory and development. Within such courses a great deal of attention has been focused on the need for, and means of formulating, aims and objectives, and history teachers are now under considerable pressure to state exactly what it is they are trying to achieve. The survey of the history syllabuses of fourteen city schools by the group of H.M.I.s (Giles 1973), for example, revealed that in nine cases there was no reference to aims and objectives, the syllabuses being simply statements of content. It was general slackness of this type that lay behind the comment of Giles that 'it seems imperative not only to re-think aims and objectives appropriate to the changing concept of the subject, but also to restate them'.

Part of the history teacher's difficulty lies in understanding exactly what is meant by the terms 'aims' and 'objectives'. In the past these have been used rather indiscriminately but today curriculum specialists are trying to define them more precisely. Thus an aim may be interpreted as a very broad statement of intent. The Open University *Humanities Foundation Course*, Unit 5 (1970), justifies history in several ways. It is stated for example that 'History enables us to know, and understand better, our fellow human beings', 'History teaches us scepticism and critical judgement' and 'History prepares us to face the problems of the contemporary world'. In the survey conducted by the Cambridge Institute of Education (1970) teachers were questioned on their 'objectives' in teaching history; the reasons they put forward included the imparting of knowledge, the stimulation of interest and curiosity, showing how the past explains the present, developing an understanding of heritage, and helping pupils identify themselves with the past. These are 'aims' rather than 'objectives'. They are statements of intent which the great majority of history teachers would accept as reasonable, and this has been the case since history teaching first became established in the nineteenth century.

Unfortunately, when related to the classroom situation, such aims tend to mean very little. Even if it were possible to measure whether there had been success in achieving the aims, this could only take place in the distant future. By that time there would be so many other variables involved – such as experience in other subjects and experience out of school – that no reliable estimate of the impact of the history course could be made. Yet in teaching we are clearly intending to achieve something, and the nature of our present society is such that we have to state exactly what it is we are trying to do and show how we measure our success. Thus curriculum theorists break aims down into objectives or statements of intent that are more meaningful in the classroom situation. The situation is complicated by the fact that there are different types of objective, but it is possible to categorise these.

Initially an aim will be broken down into a series of broad or general objectives. If the general aim is 'to show how the past explains the present', for example, a broad objective to support that aim might be 'to develop the pupil's understanding of the Northern Ireland problem'. That broad objective, which would be one of a number of similar broad objectives aimed at showing how the past explains the present, could in turn be broken down into more specific objectives. These might include 'to develop the pupil's knowledge of the geographical distribution of religious groups in Northern Ireland'; 'to explain the reasons for the partition of Ireland'; 'to examine the history of the I.R.A.', and so forth. Such objectives are still general in character but, if achieved, they bring the pupil closer towards achieving the broad objective and, ultimately, the general aim. At the same time they obviously relate much more closely to the classroom situation and are more capable of being assessed.

When related to individual lessons objectives may become very specific. The most detailed are termed 'behavioural' objectives, so called because, if they are to be achieved, they must prescribe an observable change in the behaviour of the pupil. Such an objective has clearly recognisable characteristics. It will describe what the pupil, not the teacher, is to do and give the criteria for evaluating success. It will also state the conditions under which the learning behaviour is being carried out. An example of a behavioural objective which might stem from the example of the broad objective on Northern Ireland quoted above would be: 'using a historical atlas and information contained in the textbook the pupil will be able to mark and label correctly on a blank map of Ireland the boundary of Northern Ireland and the Irish Free State and the main centres of population in Northern Ireland'. Advocates of behavioural objectives would argue that such objectives should be used to a very considerable extent and that, if the behavioural objectives were achieved, then it would follow that the broad objectives would also be achieved and progress would have been made towards the ultimate achievement of the overall aim.

A fierce debate has raged over the place objectives should occupy in curriculum planning, and many of the issues involved are relevant to history. It is argued that the use of objectives makes it easier to assess the productivity of the teacher while the act of defining an objective aids the teacher in the selection of the material and teaching methods he will employ. It is also claimed that, because the pupils are told the objectives, and can see where they are going, they can work in a more purposeful way. Supporters of teaching by objectives acknowledge the difficulties faced by teachers trying to formulate a set of objectives for their courses — for example the vast numbers that may be stated — but they point out that resource centres could make sets of objectives available for the hard-pressed teacher. Such a proposal has been canvassed in the United States, but it is not looked on favourably in Britain where it is traditional for the history teacher to remain independent in deciding his objectives.

There has been vociferous criticism of the idea of teaching history by objectives, particularly when it is taken to the extreme of behavioural objectives. This results partly from the fear that the success or failure of pupils to achieve objectives may be taken to reflect on the ability of the teacher. In this context the nineteenth-century system of 'payment by results', with all its attendant evils, is quoted as a reason against precise planning by objectives. A more substantial criticism is that it is not really possible to frame objectives to cover all aspects of the humanities subjects, including history. It may well be possible to devise objectives for physical and simple cognitive skills, such as remembering a specific number of facts or extracting information from a passage, but it is much more difficult to devise and test objectives relating to feelings and attitudes. It would be easy, for example, to frame a set of behavioural objectives on the methods of attacking and defending a motte and bailey castle but it would be far more difficult to do the same for the imaginative work that could stem from the same subject. Hence the real danger that the latter might be neglected, even though its importance is evident. The position is further complicated by the difficulty of separating high-level cognitive skills from the affective area, since these skills are increasingly concerned with the making of judgements, a process in which attitudes also play an important part. The main criticism of teaching by objectives is that there tends to be over-concentration on areas that can be most easily stated in objective terms while complex areas – particularly feelings and attitudes – are neglected. Thus, in concentrating on basic cognitive skills, it is possible to lose sight of the 'imaginative' aspect of history. In addition, in lessons planned by objectives, there may be a tendency to ignore opportunities which present themselves but which do not fit the general scheme. Thus objectives, if pushed too far, can become a straitjacket restricting individuality.

Alternative patterns to teaching purely by objectives have been suggested. An interesting approach is that described by Chanan (1974) who argues that, in the humanities, it is not established that there is an order of conceptual learning or that an 'ordered sequence of situations' can be determined. The humanities might be approached in several ways. Humanities teachers have therefore focused attention on 'stimulating *any* form of involvement with suitable subject matter', and on recognising 'any of a broad range of desirable learning outcomes, including outcomes that they could not have predicted'. Thus it may be that stated aims for lessons are deliberately general in character because the teachers see them as 'opening gambits, compared with the rapid crystallization of aims that occurs again and again, and differently each time, during the classroom encounter itself'. The teacher may, for example, have the broad intention of teaching his class about the motte and bailey castle but it may well be that during the course of the lesson the pupils' interests might lead to greater emphasis on the construction of such a fortification, or on methods of attacking or defending it, or on a more creative, imaginative or even dramatic approach to the subject. The most beneficial effect of this approach is that it seems to allow the teacher the maximum opportunity to take advantage of developments in the classroom that cannot be predicted. Even so it is still clear that the history teacher must have some objectives in mind when the lesson starts and equally he must have the capacity to recognise which educational outcomes are desirable so that, if the opportunity arises during a lesson, he can take advantage of it.

The statement of objectives both for courses and lessons is playing an increasingly important part in history teaching as it is in other subjects. Thus the history teacher should be able to recognise and state the different types of objectives and understand their place in planning the syllabus. He should appreciate that complete dependence on behavioural objectives, for example, is likely to lead to arid teaching and mental paralysis, but that such objectives do have a very worthwhile role to play in the teaching of basic skills. Although there are many difficulties involved in teaching through objectives, they are becoming very much a fact of life in the history classroom and the history teacher who ignores them does so at his peril.

The classification of objectives

It follows that if it is possible to state objectives for teaching history
it should also be possible to grade them into various categories. A
number of attempts have been made to formulate a systematic
organisation of objectives – a taxonomy – and the best known of
these is associated with the names of Bloom and Krathwohl. In his
earlier work Bloom (1956) divided educational objectives into three
'domains', the cognitive, affective and psychomotor. He concerned
himself primarily with the cognitive domain while Krathwohl concentrated on the affective. Bloom worked on the basis that, in
thinking about a problem or topic, a hierarchy of cognitive processes
is involved. He defined six main classes in the hierarchy, each higher
step encompassing those below. These were, in ascending order of
difficulty, knowledge, comprehension, application, analysis, synthesis and evaluation. The simplest – knowledge – was defined as
'little more than the remembering of the idea or phenomenon in a
form very close to that in which it was originally encountered'. The
units themselves were capable of subdivision so that analysis, for
example, comprised analysis of elements, of relationships and of
organisational relationships. In the same way Krathwohl (1964)
provided a hierarchy for the affective domain which took as
organising themes receiving (attending), responding, valuing,
organisation and characterisation by a value or a value complex.

Bloom's taxonomy was intended as a guide for teachers of all subjects, helping them to establish which levels of thinking they were
trying to promote, and to select the relevant teaching methods,
resources and forms of evaluation. Complications arise in using it
because the discipline of history does not lend itself to subdivision in
this way. Thus the history specialist has to select that which is relevant in the work of Bloom and Krathwohl to his main task – the communication to his pupils of an understanding of the nature and
methods of history. There have been a number of attempts to do this
but by far the most influential has been the taxonomy produced by
Coltham and Fines (1971). This has proved a work of fundamental
importance for English history teachers as it has formed a basis for

much that has happened since in many schools. Using Bloom's taxonomy as a basis, Coltham and Fines formulated a much simplified hierarchy in which the bias is still towards the behaviour of the learner. Objectives were thus grouped under a framework containing four main headings, each of which is subdivided:

A *Attitudes towards the study of history*
   1 Attending
   2 Responding
   3 Imagining

B *Nature of the discipline*
   1 Nature of information
   2 Organising procedures
   3 Products

C *Skills and abilities*
   1 Vocabulary acquisition
   2 Reference skills
   3 Memorisation
   4 Comprehension
   5 Translation
   6 Analysis
   7 Extrapolation
   8 Synthesis
   9 Judgment and evaluation
  10 Communication skills

D *Educational outcomes of study*
   1 Insight
   2 Knowledge of values
   3 Reasoned judgment

Section C deals in detail with the cognitive domain (the skills and abilities necessary for understanding the subject), while Section A is concerned with attitudes towards the subject. Section B is related to the nature of the subject in which the skills and abilities will be employed and towards which the attitudes will be formed, while Section D brings the previous three sections together in terms of what may be contributed to the development of the person who is learning. In practice the four sections are very closely interrelated, but, although artificial, it is clearly useful for planning purposes to separate out the main themes at a theoretical level.

It is very important for the history teacher to have a clear understanding of the way in which it was intended that the taxonomy should be used. It was certainly never seen as a prescription which had to be taken in its entirety. Coltham (1972) emphasised that it should be seen as a 'working document', helping teachers to plan and assess their courses. The taxonomy could be used in one of two ways. It might be seen as a guide in the planning stage of a course so that the teacher could select objectives in the areas he considered important and then relate these to teaching strategies, resources, etc. Alternatively the taxonomy could be used to evaluate existing courses, the teacher selecting those elements of the taxonomy he considered important and using them as a checklist against his courses. Even the taxonomy itself was not seen as a final model but was viewed as a document that would be worked on and modified in the light of the experience gained.

The Coltham and Fines taxonomy is full of interest for the history teacher. It can certainly help the teacher to plan his courses more effectively. On the other hand the teacher has to beware of the danger of over-concentration on the achievement of specific skills or the development of particular attitudes, so losing sight of the real quarry, the development of the pupil's insight into history. Further, it is probable that other subjects will also evolve their own taxonomies which, at a general level, are unlikely to be very different from the example quoted for history. Thus, as Giles and Neal (1973) have commented, there is a real danger that the subject may languish into 'detached handfuls' – joined with 'handfuls' of other disciplines – each isolated to foster an identical skill. Much depends on the initiative of the individual history teacher and, in particular, on his ability to use the taxonomy as an instrument in planning courses.

In this context the work of Palmer (1973) in Leicestershire provides an interesting insight into the problems facing the history teacher who tries to make the teaching of the subject more effective. She is keenly aware of the wider issues involved in teaching history, such as the importance of attitudes – particularly with regard to

older children. Yet the two archive teaching units with which he\
name is associated — 'Law and Order in Leicestershire' and 'Leicestershire Farming' — are geared very much to the development of cognitive abilities, partly because the teacher has more opportunity to assess these. Thus using the Coltham and Fines taxonomy as a basis and drawing on her own wide experience of observing children working on archive material, Palmer selected comprehension, translation, analysis, synthesis, recognition, inference-making and evaluation as the abilities that could be most encouraged through the use of sources and this is reflected in the units. Palmer's work is highly encouraging because it shows a willingness to use the taxonomy in the way in which it was intended — as an aid to clarify the thinking of the teacher. At the same time it does reveal the dangers involved, in particular the tendency to emphasise the cognitive aspects and to assume that, if there is cognitive development, there is less need to pay close attention to the affective area.

Conclusion

The formulation and classification of objectives is likely to play an increasingly important part in teaching and history teachers are finding that they need to be very much more precise in defining what they are trying to achieve. They must beware, however, of the dangers of concentrating on that which can be most easily measured, the acquisition of knowledge and the development of cognitive skills. Similarly they must see a taxonomy as an aid and therefore use it, rather than allow it to become a straitjacket limiting their freedom. Even more important is the fact that teachers must not see the use of objectives in isolation. The formulation and classification of objectives must relate closely to what is understood of the development of the child's thinking, the statement of cognitive objectives, for example, taking into account the child's capacity to think at a concrete or formal operational level of thought. Above all it must be acknowledged that the primary purpose is to develop the child's understanding of the nature and methods of history and it is this that gives unity to the whole exercise.

5 Examinations and history teaching

One of the byproducts of the growing preoccupation with planning through objectives is the increased emphasis given to assessment; as a result there has been a much closer scrutiny in recent years of the effect of the examination system on history teaching. This development is to be welcomed, though it should not be overlooked that examinations have been analysed in the past and many of their limitations have been recognised and commented on. A Cambridge don and local examiner noted as early as 1877 that:

Examiners are often driven to give up as hopeless the attempt to test directly the real good got by the study – the quality of the kernel itself – but they try to judge of it by scrutinising the husk – they ask questions of facts and dates, they ask for genealogies and 'short summaries', but these are just what the man who profits most cannot give them, and what the man who has 'got up' the subject . . . has at his finger tips. (Latham 1877)

The bulk of the criticism of examining in history at O level today is similar in tone to Latham's comments, and G.C.E. history has become a byword for monotony and boredom. The original London University history matriculation paper, set in 1838, required candidates to answer twelve essay questions set on an outline English history syllabus in three hours. Today the nine G.C.E. examining boards set papers which still have much in common with those set in the nineteenth century. The majority of O level papers for example are set on an outline English or European history syllabus and require that four or five essay questions be answered in two and a half hours. Even the wording of the questions has changed little, although the number to be answered has been reduced.

The effect of the O level history examination on the teaching of the subject throughout the school has been drastic. The prescription of a syllabus for the fourth and fifth years has automatic implications for the construction of the syllabus lower down the school. Similarly the use of the essay as the basis of the examination has led to a concentration on essay writing in the classroom and the inevitable corollary of this is that other approaches – oral work, field work, projects, etc. – have been undervalued and underemployed. The dependence on the essay has also led to excessive concentration on note-taking and, in particular, to the dictation of notes so that the pupil can prepare more thoroughly for the examination. The reverberations of this have echoed all the way down to the first form. It is a sad comment on the state of the subject that books of printed notes and model answers have proved a commercially viable proposition, for they represent the very antithesis of the nature of history. Fortunately the outlook is not completely black and there are encouraging signs of change. The stimulus for these, however, has come largely from the introduction of the Certificate of Secondary Education (C.S.E.) during the early 1960s.

The impact of the C.S.E. on the examination system

The C.S.E. is a comparatively recent innovation, the first examination papers having been set in 1965. In all there are fourteen C.S.E. examining boards which set papers for the 40 per cent, in ability terms, of the school population below the 20 per cent which are entered for G.C.E. The schools opt for one of three types of examination. In Mode I, which is by far the most common, the history panel of the board prescribes the syllabus and examines the pupils. In Mode II the school sets its own syllabus, and this is examined externally. In Mode III the school again sets its own syllabus, but also undertakes the responsibility of examining it and the C.S.E. history board appoints a moderator.

The inclination of the schools towards selecting Mode I is interesting. The roots of this lie, in many ways, in the difficulties of implementing Modes II and III. In Mode III the teachers have an increased workload – they have to produce their own syllabus and decide on their own form of internal assessment – and many of the younger teachers lack the experience and confidence to do this. Further, Mode III involves planning, discussion and gaining the approval of the board well in advance of the course's starting, and consequently the process is long and time-consuming. Even so one board – West Yorkshire and Lindsey – has succeeded in encouraging a much higher proportion of schools than normal to opt for Mode III history. In that region there is an active policy of encouraging Mode III partly by streamlining procedures for the presentation of syllabuses and examination details. As a result approximately 70 per cent of candidates in history are entered under Mode III (Bucknall 1974) whereas, at a national level, the figure is less than 10 per cent.

At first sight the variety of papers set by the C.S.E. boards is bewildering. Docking (1970) researched the examining of history at this level. He found for example that the East Midlands offered seventeen syllabuses under Mode I and East Anglia sixteen, but that the North and Metropolitan Boards set only two and Yorkshire three. The differing philosophies of the boards led to this variation, those offering just a few options taking the line that schools could offer their own syllabuses under Modes II and III if they wanted alternatives. It is interesting that this proved not to be the case and boards offering a limited choice under Mode I did not find a significantly higher proportion of schools opting for Modes II and III. In all the boards it was also noticeable that there was a heavy emphasis on modern world history and British social and economic history since 1750.

One of the great advantages enjoyed by the C.S.E. boards is that, being relatively new, they are not restricted by tradition. Another important factor is that teachers have been encouraged to play a full part in the work of the boards. As a result there has been a much more enlightened approach to the examination of pupils in history at this level. It has certainly led to an interesting paradox. Because

C.S.E. candidates were thought less able than their G.C.E. counter-parts to digest the conclusions of the professional historian, a different approach has been adopted to their teaching and assessment. C.S.E. pupils have been encouraged to pursue their own inquiries and to use a range of sources other than the textbook. Thus documents, pictures, photographs, cartoons, maps, statistics, graphs, and the like, have loomed much larger in the diet of the C.S.E. pupil and, ironically, he has thus been working much more in the style of the professional historian. The essay still plays a prominent role in the C.S.E. and this is understandable since it does test certain cognitive skills. C.S.E. boards do offer more guidance on answering essay questions, however, as they frequently provide subheadings which give the candidate a clearer idea of the content required. Also significant are the other forms of question asked which allow the less literate student to demonstrate his ability. Thus short-answer and multiple-choice objective-type questions may be employed. Questions based on documentary material may be set, or candidates required to analyse statistics or graphs, or draw inferences from photographs, pictures or cartoons. Such questions are clearly more 'concrete' in character and are calculated to test a much greater range of abilities than the standard essay-based examination.

THE PERSONAL TOPIC
The most striking effect of the introduction of the C.S.E. in history has been the success of the personal topic. Many of the boards allocate a proportion of the marks, usually within the range 20–40 per cent, for course work. Eight of the fourteen boards require the production of a personal topic, usually between 2,000 and 3,000 words, and in five it is optional. The North Regional Board in fact requires a length of 3,000–8,000 words, and the examiner has the right to visit the schools in question in order to discuss the projects with the candidates and check their interest and understanding. The background to the development of the personal topic has been fully explored by the Schools Council (Examination Bulletin No 18, 1968). The topic was viewed in a very favourable light in that, although the teachers encountered many difficulties—lack of resources, problems in

arranging visits and of supervision, shortage of time, complications in assessment, etc. – they were also able to identify 'some very real advantages such as marked enthusiasm, stimulated interest, greater understanding of the subject, a wish to continue its study, and a feeling that something had really been learnt and something achieved'.

The introduction of the personal study is an advance of basic importance in history teaching. The Schools Council publication referred to above recorded that teachers were more interested in the personal topics as an educational process than as a mode of assessment and thus by its very nature the personal study comes much closer than the essay-based examination to achieving the objectives of the history teacher. The candidate is required to show evidence of research, of reading around the subject and of understanding. He is expected to present the study in his own words, explain his choice of topic and comment on its value. Such a task is much more demanding than the standard essay, but it is much more akin to the work of the professional historian or the university or college student writing a thesis or producing a local study. It provides scope for the less academically gifted pupil to produce a personal topic in which he is interested, because there is a greater opportunity for creative and imaginative work and because presentation may be in a variety of forms other than the written word – tape recordings, visual illustration, photographs, etc. A word of caution is also necessary however. If the teacher does not have a clear idea of the objectives of doing a personal project and fails to communicate them to his pupils, the project can become an even more protracted and unproductive slog than the essay-based examination. Indeed there is no shortage of evidence that in many instances pupils copy large extracts from books and accumulate a mass of unused information. The key to success rests with the teacher's capacity to understand what he is trying to achieve and his ability to communicate his ideas to the pupils.

The impact of the C.S.E. on the G.C.E.

The impact of the C.S.E. on the G.C.E. is becoming increasingly evident, although the process is a very slow one. In the past the G.C.E. boards have paid lip service to the idea of innovation by declaring a willingness to consider alternative syllabuses submitted by interested schools. In practice all the pressures – lack of time, the need to plan well in advance of change, difficulty in securing approval for a syllabus, and so on – have combined to restrict the development of new approaches, and it is only during the past ten years that there have been significant changes.

In common with the universities, and with the C.S.E. boards, the G.C.E. boards are tending to widen their syllabuses and examine both world and modern British social and economic history. They are also experimenting with examination papers which vary in form from the more traditional essay-based approach. Much interesting work in this area has been done by Macintosh (1971), whose name is closely associated with the development of objective tests in history. Macintosh assisted the A.E.B. in devising suitable objectives and forms of assessment for its O level Economic and Social History syllabus. The examination paper, which was produced in consultation with teachers, included a multiple-choice objective test, questions based on stimulus material, and essays. Similarly in 1974 the London Board paper on English/European History 1760–1955 made use of three techniques in assessment: the multiple-choice objective test, questions based on source material, and structured-essay questions.

The extent of the change in G.C.E. history, however, should not be exaggerated. The great majority of pupils still take examinations that are traditional in character. They continue to study outline British or European history syllabuses, and to answer essay-based examination papers. A strong measure of support for this approach still survives and in 1972 for instance Gasson and Stokes noted of G.C.E. questions that they should be unambiguous and that 'in most instances there is only one answer'. The irony here is that, if teachers work towards this end, they are trying to achieve an objective which is against the interests of the subject. Stenhouse (1975) has explained the depressing similarity of history essays by noting:

the majority of teachers have been working to a behavioural objective – to produce just such an essay. They don't talk about objectives because they feel they are rather disreputable, but they are using them. From the pile of essays a few leap out at the marker as original, surprising, showing evidence of individual thinking. These, the unpredictable, are the successes. In the university setting, they are the ones who get the firsts.

While it is undeniable that questions should be unambiguous, it seems a denial of the nature of the subject for there to be only one possible answer to a historical question. Gasson and Stokes also suggest that candidates prepare for the G.C.E. by doing questions at home so as to avoid taking up time in class. This raises the rather fundamental point that, if more worthwhile activities are planned for the classroom, surely these – and not just skill in essay writing – should form the basis of the examination.

The most encouraging improvements in G.C.E. history have been when individual teachers, or groups of teachers, have approached the boards with a view to developing their own syllabuses and papers. Jones (1972) has described how the Oxford Local Examination Board approved a history syllabus on Medieval European History 325–1250 which included an individual project as part of the assessment, at Maidstone Grammar School. In 1966 this was accepted as an official Mode III O level with 40 per cent of the marks being allocated to the project and 60 per cent to an examination paper. The paper was also set by the school, the board reviser selecting eight from ten to twelve submitted questions, and the candidates being required to answer three in one and a half hours. The most interesting feature of the scheme was that the interest in project work percolated down through the school, and much of the lower school work was organised on a project basis. This characteristic has also been observed in other schools including a project as part of their G.C.E. assessment (Milne 1973).

A final example of the value of individual initiative in the approach to O level examinations is provided by the work of Roberts (1972) as head of the history department at Brays Grove Comprehensive School, Harlow. Roberts related the taxonomy devised by Coltham and Fines to the European History 1870–1955 O level syllabus then taken in the school and found numerous deficiencies. He concluded that the declared school aims were so vague or long term that they could not be assessed, and that the intellectual skills particularly encouraged by the examination – memorisation and synthesis – dominated the teaching. Consequently, under the aegis of the Cambridge University Local Examinations Syndicate, a new syllabus was devised, geared to the achievement of certain cognitive and affective objectives, and this was first examined, on a Mode III basis, in 1973. 25 per cent of the marks were allocated for a project, 25 per cent for course work, and 50 per cent for a final examination paper which was divided into three sections, each testing different levels of skills. The attempt to test attitudinal objectives, through the production of a personal project, is a striking comment on the success of the project in the C.S.E. Equally, Roberts's innovation is particularly worthy of note because it reflects a systematic attempt to build in teacher-formulated objectives into a public examination, instead of allowing the examination itself to dictate the objectives.

Conclusion

Although O level history remains a monotonous grind for many pupils, there are encouraging signs in the examination of the subject. This is reflected in Part II in the descriptions by Kirby and Roberts of the mixed mode O level at the Graham Balfour High School, Stafford, and White of the C.S.E. Mode III at Clough Hall Comprehensive School, Kidsgrove. As the emphasis on a systematic formulation of objectives becomes more pronounced, so the inadequacies of traditional forms of examination are revealed. Teachers are becoming increasingly aware that they are concerned with the development of the intellectual skills and attitudes that make the study of history a meaningful exercise, and that these must be defined before the form of the examination can be decided upon. It seems likely, for example, that the majority of pupils who maintain an interest in history when they leave school will watch historical programmes, read historical material or discuss historical issues. It is certainly less likely that they will write historical essays. They should therefore be encouraged to watch and read with understanding, to find and analyse evidence for themselves and should be trained to discuss issues intelligently. A greater emphasis on oral work in examinations may therefore be called for. The key point is that the examination is simply the instrument used to establish whether the objectives are being achieved. It must be the servant rather than the master; hopefully, history teachers are becoming more aware of this, but there is certainly no room for complacency.

6 Classroom strategies

See p. 2
Quote

The shape of the history syllabus

THE CHRONOLOGICAL-OUTLINE SYLLABUS
The chronological-outline syllabus remains by far the most widely used. The Cambridge Institute Enquiry (1970) found that 77 per cent of all schools within the region followed a broad chronological pattern in teaching history to the eleven to fourteen age group. Pupils following such a syllabus would normally work through, at a very superficial level, from the Stone Age to as near the present as they could get. In a typical secondary school the first years would cover the period from the Stone Age to the Roman occupation, the second year would work through from the Anglo-Saxons to the Wars of the Roses, and the third year would tackle the Tudors and Stuarts. The fourth and fifth years would be devoted largely to examination work with a heavy emphasis on either political, or social and economic, British or European history from approximately 1750.

In the nineteenth century the study of the chronological outline was seen as an essential preparation for the later study of history. An elementary school teacher would have worked through the outline three times in his career, first as a pupil in school, then as a pupil-teacher, and finally as a college student. It was believed that, once the outline was firmly established in the mind, a foundation had then been laid for later studies in depth. A second reason why it was considered worthwhile to follow a chronological approach was that it was believed that history was concerned with evolution, a continuous process of which the children should be aware. Further, it was accepted that Britain was progressing (the 'dark ages' were being left behind, etc.), and the pupil should develop a sense of pride in his country's achievements. These were the ideas which appealed to the examining boards when they were first drawing up their history syllabuses and the consequences are still with us. In their desperate attempt to get through the syllabus and cover all events of major importance, teachers have largely ignored children's interests. They have concentrated on ensuring that their pupils acquire the basic information and a sense of time, and their methods have been designed to achieve this end. Thus, although chronological-outline syllabus is logical in its construction, it is weak in that it ignores the psychological aspects of learning, and much of the current criticism of history teaching can be traced to its influence.

THE PATCH-ERA-TOPIC APPROACH

Varying definitions of these approaches to syllabus construction may be found, but they do have much in common – in particular the view that pupils benefit from making a more detailed study of shorter periods. These need not necessarily be closely related in time, although an understanding of chronology within the period is important. The scale of the study may vary and the pupil may be concerned for instance with life in general in Elizabethan England or more specifically with an event such as the Spanish Armada. The intention would be for the theme studied to be viewed from a range of angles and a more complex concept established, while at the same time the pupil would be more encouraged to project himself back into the past than he would be following an outline approach. In studying a patch-era type of syllabus the pupil is also more likely to be working in the style of the historian in that, instead of concentrating on those aspects of the past that are relevant to the present, as is likely in studying an outline syllabus, the pupil will be more concerned with the reconstruction of the past in its own right.

The patch-era-topic type approach does require a higher level of understanding. It demands more work on the part of the teacher and the use of a greater range of resources – books, visual aids, etc. It is thus somewhat ironic that the approach has been used most widely in the past in junior schools where the children would appear to be less well equipped mentally to achieve all that is hoped for in the study of a period in depth. The introduction of the personal topic in the C.S.E. and G.C.E., however, does indicate that the advantages of working in this way are becoming more widely appreciated in the secondary schools.

THE LINE OF DEVELOPMENT

A third approach to syllabus construction, largely associated with the work of Jeffreys in the 1930s, is the 'line of development'. Like the project, this is more popular in junior schools, but it has found a place in secondary schools. The idea of chronology is basic to the line of development, Jeffreys believing that 'the peculiar contribution of historical study to our outlook is the developmental perspective – the habit of seeing events in evolutionary relations, the whole process being assumed to be one of growth and not of mere succession' (1939). Jeffreys overcame the problem of selection from the mass of historical material available by picking relevant themes and developing them on a chronological basis. The pupil therefore follows a course in which he studies themes – the home, education, medicine, transport, etc. – and traces their development through the ages. Jeffreys anticipated that, by the end of the course, an integrated understanding of the past would be achieved through the study of a number of suitably cross-referenced themes.

The line of development has much to recommend it. The definition of subject matter is easy and it is certainly a study in depth, of a kind. The themes can also be based on the pupils' interests. There are complications, however, which must not be overlooked. The difficulties of children in understanding time have already been pointed out. Moreover, within any period many factors may produce change. It would be difficult, for example, to do justice to the development of transport in the eighteenth century without ranging more widely in the period than a line of development on transport through the ages would permit. In addition, history is concerned with establishing the uniqueness of the past. It is difficult to see how pupils can reasonably be expected to put together a coherent picture of the past at the end of a course comprising a series of outlines.

THE REGRESSIVE APPROACH

First advocated in the nineteenth century, the 'regressive' approach commands considerable attention today. Some confusion surrounds the term and it has been interpreted for example as starting with what is familiar to the child and working towards the unfamiliar. Much more commonly accepted, however, is the idea that a regressive approach means starting a study in the present and tracing its development back into the past – thus reversing the natural order. It is an approach that is being quite widely canvassed at the present time. Stacey (1969), for example, suggested taking a contemporary event such as the Russian invasion of Czechoslovakia and tracing its origins back to both the creation of Czechoslovakia after the First World War and the Russian Revolution. Similarly a B.B.C. radio programme for 1975–6, 'History: Not So Long Ago', was based on a regressive principle, while much of the work in family and local history also starts in the present and works back into the past.

It is suggested that, because the regressive approach starts with a contemporary issue or problem, the syllabus is more 'relevant' to the pupil and he will therefore be more motivated towards its study. Further, it is argued that, if the pupil can understand a topic in its contemporary setting, he will be better able to understand it in the past. There are elements of truth in these points but there are also dangers which should not be underestimated. If pupils commence the study of history by studying contemporary society there is a serious chance of historical distortion, since the interests and values of present-day society are not necessarily the same as those of the past. The primary aim of the study of history is, using historical methods, to establish the uniqueness of past events, and it is questionable whether the regressive approach, with its strong emphasis on the present, facilitates this. It would also be a mistake to assume that any theme significant in contemporary society which has a historical perspective will be seen as 'relevant' by the pupil. Psychological factors must be taken into account and it may well be that themes from the distant past will be seen by pupils as being as more 'relevant' to their needs.

Clearly the history teacher in planning his courses has to make decisions about the shape of the syllabus and his task is not easy. The basis of his choice must rest with his ability to define his aims and objectives in teaching history. If the teacher's intention is to give a synoptic view of the past, the chronological outline or line of development is obviously most suitable. If the intention is to explain the present, then the regressive syllabus would seem to be appropriate. If the objective is to get the pupil to work in the style of the historian and to develop his ability to project himself back into the past, the patch-era-topic-based syllabus is likely to be most suitable. The essential point is that different shapes of syllabuses serve different purposes, and it is very much the individual responsibility of the teacher to decide which to use.

Changes in the content of the history syllabus

Just as the shape of the history syllabus has come in for close scrutiny during recent years, so too has the content. Gradually English and European political, social and economic history is giving ground, while new areas are competing for a foothold in the syllabus. In particular the rival claims of world and contemporary as against local history are being pushed very strongly.

WORLD AND CONTEMPORARY HISTORY

Frequently there is confusion over the terms 'world history' and 'contemporary history' and sometimes the two are taken to mean the same thing. In reality they are different, as are the arguments for their inclusion in the history syllabus. World history should be seen as the evolution of mankind, without temporal or spatial limits. In contrast, contemporary history, although it has no spatial limits, is restricted to the recent past. Contemporary history may therefore be seen as part of world history, but world history need not be contemporary history.

The progress of the world and contemporary history movement

has been dramatic. Heater (1968) expressed the opinion that: 'The construction of courses in Contemporary World History has probably been the most significant single development in the subject in the 1960s.' The momentum has been maintained during the 1970s. A world or contemporary history element is compulsory in the syllabus of the History 13–16 Project, and all fourteen of the C.S.E. boards offer a Mode I syllabus in world history. Such evidence as is available in the schools – although it tends to be very fragmentary – points in the same direction. A survey of schools in the Birmingham/Dudley area in 1975, for example, found that almost 40 per cent of the schools that replied to a questionnaire were teaching world history topics for half or more of the history timetable. (I am indebted for this reference to John Robottom, Midlands Education Officer of the Schools Broadcasting Council.) Such facts and figures reflect the increasing prestige of contemporary and world history and there are good reasons for their increasing popularity.

The advocates of world history see its study as contributing to the development of an international rather than a national outlook, and believe that it should help to prepare students for world citizenship. Strotzka (1971), an Austrian teacher, commented that: 'We are living in a world which has so spectacularly been unified by science and technology and by means of mass communications, that it would be futile to limit our interest to such a small entity as a nation.' Thus he recognised the need to transcend man's limited outlook and claimed: 'The unique quality of teaching world history lies in coming into contact with different outlooks, and its purpose is to see the impact of other civilisations on our own.' The arguments in favour of contemporary history are rather different. It is most commonly justified on the grounds that it is more 'relevant' to the pupil, i.e. it is seen as being much closer to the pupil's needs and hence he is presumed to be more likely to be favourably disposed towards its study. It is also assumed that if the pupil is better informed on the contemporary world he will be better fitted to take his place in it. In this context Burrell (1972) noted that 'history teaching can best meet the demand that is should be relevant if courses enable students to understand themselves and the age in which they live, and this means, above all, a study of the recent past at some time in their secondary career.' He therefore recommended the inclusion of contemporary European studies in the history syllabus.

The movement towards world and contemporary history has to be seen against the backcloth of Britain's declining role in the world. It must also be viewed against a background of discontent with the effects of teaching more nationally based history. It is important to remember, though, that national history has been taught largely through traditional, examination-orientated methods, and if world or contemporary history is approached in the same way the effects are likely to be even more damaging to the interests of the subject. As we have seen, history teaching in the past has been criticised for its lack of attention to the pupil's ability to understand the subject matter, the mechanical methods by which it was introduced to the pupil, and the employment of arid forms of assessment. The same could well prove true of the teaching of world or contemporary history. The scope of the study is global, while the pupil's geographical awareness is likely to be limited. The quantity of material available for study is vast and – even with careful selection – the dangers of oversimplification are real. To what extent can a sixteen-year-old come to terms with the Vietnam War without having a grasp of the ideological complexities involved? Is it not likely that the varying interpretations of the progress of the U.S.S.R. since 1917 demand a level of understanding well beyond that of the average fifth-former? It is evident that if traditional methods of teaching and assessment continue to be employed and subject matter is selected without careful thought as to the pupil's capacity to understand it, the teaching of world and contemporary history is likely to be subject to just as much criticism as the teaching of national history in the past.

It also follows, however, that if world and contemporary history can be made interesting and worthwhile through the use of more enlightened teaching methods, the same could be said for national history. Thus, in selecting the content of his syllabus, the teacher has to work from his aims and objectives in teaching history. It may well prove to be the case that the various branches of history – social, economic, political, local, world, etc. – have a distinctive contribution to make to the historical education of the pupil. World history, for example, might bring a global perspective to history which the other areas cannot. Contemporary history may be claimed to be more 'relevant', although there is considerable confusion in the use of the term. In this context it should mean that the topic studied is relevant to the understanding of present-day issues. Undoubtedly world and contemporary history do have an important contribution to make in the historical education of the pupil. There is also a wealth of good audio-visual material to support their study – an important point in relation to the latest pedagogical theories and the new history teaching strategies. Yet, on their own, world and contemporary do not present a panacea for the ills of history teaching. They must be viewed as an integral part of a coherent history syllabus, perhaps on the lines of that laid down by the Schools Council History 13–16 Project, which includes elements of local, national and international history.

LOCAL AND ENVIRONMENTAL HISTORY

A second area in which there is growing interest in schools is local and environmental history, but the progress made in introducing this subject to pupils is by no means as impressive as in the case of world and contemporary studies. This is rather surprising as the integrity of local history as a legitimate area of study is now unquestioned. Hoskins (1967) has done much to overthrow the 'parish pump' image of the subject and has given some indication of the intellectual rigour required in its study:

There is no opposition between fieldwork and documents. Both are essential to the good local historian. Behind a good deal of work in the field and the street are documents that help to throw more light on what is being studied; and behind a good many documents lies much fieldwork if only the unimaginative 'researchers' had the wit to see it.

As the modern trend in history teaching is to get the pupil, whatever his age, to work more in the style of the professional historian, the advocates of local history feel their subject has a special case to be included in the school curriculum. Douch (1970) has pointed out the need for children to be involved in history and that they should see it 'not as a film which they simply watch, but as a continuing play in which they themselves are actors'. Preston (1969) has argued that the study of local history helps to give pupils both a sense of the past and a greater understanding of the present, and that 'It provides real contact, tangible evidence and concrete history far removed from the text-book. As such it can ... transform history from "dull and boring" to active and practical.' Cook (1970) sees yet another advantage in including local history in the syllabus in that 'by its study the educative process is transferred from the classroom to the world of reality and thus the teacher becomes a guide and active participator rather than an academic tutor'.

In spite of the strong arguments in its favour, the position of local history is still relatively weak. Initially its main impact was in primary schools and the Plowden Report (1967), for example, attributed the increased interest in history to the use of projects which took children out of the classroom and involved them in fieldwork in the local environment. More recently, at a secondary level, the introduction of the personal topic in the C.S.E. has encouraged the study of locally based topics. Progress has been limited, however, as was shown by the results of a 1970 survey into the use of fieldwork in history teaching in the secondary schools of one Midland county (Roots 1970). Roots found that in over half the schools there was no history fieldwork, nor were there any special centres to encourage it. Further, there was little cooperation between schools and local history societies, archaeological societies, museums or libraries. Where there was activity it usually took the form of day visits to stately homes or to places of local interest and, even then, pre-visit preparation was limited as some teachers seemed to be reluctant to 'spoil an enjoyable day out by asking for some work to be done'.

The reasons for the weakness of local history in school are not hard to find. The teacher's attitude to the subject is critical and, invariably, he is the prisoner of his own experience. Because he tends not to encounter local history in university or college courses the teacher does not develop the expertise in the area that would give him the confidence to introduce it in the classroom. For the inexperienced teacher local history can be alarming in its demands. Fieldwork skills are required as well as a knowledge of the vast range of local history sources available in libraries, museums and record offices. The teacher can only appreciate the pedagogical implications of local history when he has gained some mastery over the subject. Thus it is that, although local history probably lends itself to a greater variety of approaches in school than any other branch of history, it has failed to make the progress that it should. Instead, the gap left in schools by the decline of the more traditional British and European outline history syllabuses has been filled more by world and contemporary history, and this would seem to be a reflection of the same tendency in universities.

Evolving techniques

The methods employed by the history teacher are bound to reflect his aims and objectives in teaching the subject. In the past the teacher's main objective seems to have been the passing of O level history – as is evidenced by the heavy concentration on chalk and talk, insistence on a good set of notes, dependence on a single textbook, determination to cover the whole syllabus, constant practice in essay writing, and emphasis on factual recall. Ironically the use of these techniques did not necessarily mean that an O level pass was achieved – as is indicated by the relatively high failure rate. Their use today can contribute even less to the achievement of the aims and objectives that are now being stated for history teaching. Increasingly teachers are concerned with the attitudes of their pupils towards the subject, and with the pupils' acquisition of the skills involved in its study. Inevitably this has important implications for the teaching techniques employed and the resources used, and significant changes are taking place.

THE USE OF SOURCE MATERIAL IN THE CLASSROOM

The most striking development of the past twenty years has been the acceptance of the idea that the pupil should work in the style of the professional historian. This was given academic responsibility by the argument of Bruner (1968) that it is possible for the schoolchild, at any age, to learn something of the structure of the subject in question. An interesting example suggesting that infants may think in the same way as the professional historian, though at their own level, was given by Stenhouse (1975) when he suggested that the infant class considering the origins of a playground fight and a historian analysing the origins of the First World War were essentially engaged in the same sort of task, i.e. they were attempting to understand the event using concepts of causation, etc. Most attention has centred, however, on the use of historical sources in the classroom and their possible role in developing thinking skills.

The idea of using source material in the classroom is by no means new. Payne (1875) advocated a more scientific approach to history in the classroom, in particular through the use of original sources. The use of historical sources to develop thinking skills, however, is really a phenomenon of the past twenty years. In 1957 Batho developed a series of 'archive teaching units' — a collection of facsimiles of original documents and materials on a selected theme, for example Mary Queen of Scots. Archive units now number hundreds and vary enormously in structure and form, some, such as the series produced by Tyson at Newcastle upon Tyne, being sophisticated in their educational coherence. The rapid increase in the number of 'Jackdaw' kits also reflects the growth in popularity of the source method, as does the use of archive materials in conjunction with radio and television programmes. The radio programme 'History in Evidence' is based on the use of archive and documentary material, and the television series 'British Social History' and 'History 1917–73' are based on the use of archive film and sources. Even examinations reflect the trend, the papers of the West Yorkshire and Lindsey Board for example containing questions based on documentary extracts or other source material – photographs, statistics, maps and diagrams, etc. (Bucknall 1974).

In using source or archive material the pupil is working much more in the style of the historian, but there are important differences. The professional historian has to decide on his area of research, locate all the relevant sources, and use them as he considers appropriate. In contrast, unless the pupil is working independently on a project, the teacher or producer of the archive unit has already made the selection for him and the pupil may exercise only limited choice. On the other hand, in using the documents, etc., he may well be able to acquire and develop such important skills as the detection of prejudice or bias, or the establishment of the veracity or authenticity of documents. Thus current educational aspirations may be fulfilled. Certainly the use of sources demands that the pupils be more active. Equally pupils are learning how to learn and there is less danger of their acquiring a body of information which will quickly become obsolete and useless. It is anticipated in fact that through the development of thinking skills the pupil will be better able to adapt to the changing needs of society in the future.

The use of sources in the classroom in order to develop thinking skills, combined with their other roles of providing atmosphere and illustration, does raise many questions, and Batho (1972) has focused attention on these. The most important point is that practice in the use of sources has outstripped thinking about their use. Batho points out how much energy and time have been spent on the production of archive units, without any corresponding basic research as to the form in which they might best be presented, how far source materials should be presented by the teacher, whether visual materials are more worthwhile than verbal, whether an archive unit should concern itself with a basic problem or be more wide-ranging, and so on. As Wood (1973) has pointed out, there is a danger that archive units, because they are successful, may become a new kind of orthodoxy – a different kind of 'textbook'. Undoubtedly sources are being introduced on an increasingly wide scale in the classroom and it is incumbent on teachers to think through the implications of using the source method so that they can gain the maximum benefit from their efforts.

Concern with the use of sources and with developing activity methods in teaching history has also contributed to the opening up of interesting new approaches to the subject in schools, for example demography and family history, games and simulations, and drama.

These should be seen as complementing one another rather than as providing a complete historical education in themselves, but each certainly has a worthwhile contribution to make to the education of the pupil.

DEMOGRAPHY AND FAMILY HISTORY

References to demography and family history have become increasingly common in recent years. Although the two tend to be bracketed together there are significant differences between them. The case for demography has been best argued by Turner (1974), who has suggested that it should appear at short but regular intervals in the history curriculum and that it might be approached in a variety of ways. Thus the distribution of population in the past – and related factors like migration or occupations – might be studied. Alternatively a detailed study might be made of a local community using, for example, population sources and statistics in conjunction with changes in agricultural practice. A sociological approach could use population statistics to explore 'the numerical and qualitative differences between families of different classes, their wealth, age at marriage, the size of their family and of their house'. The pupils might also follow an economic approach, linking population and prices, or a medical approach linking such factors as epidemics and birth control to population size and structure. The use of population data in schools demands careful preparation and has to be closely related to the pupil's capacity to understand it. Nevertheless, the difficulties are not insuperable and such material has been used effectively at junior and secondary levels. In using demographic material, albeit at his own level, the pupil is working in the style of the professional historian; this represents a distinct advance in methodology.

The same could well be said of family history, an area that is gaining in popularity. A carefully argued case for its inclusion in the curriculum has been put forward by Steel and Taylor (1971). Family history is seen as particularly relevant to the classroom because it draws on the pupil's experience and because it is an area he is likely to consider important. Moreover the study of his family requires that the pupil be active in that he must locate the relevant evidence and use it in order to reach conclusions. As Steel and Taylor noted:

> it cannot be emphasised enough, that the primary aim is for the child to engage in an historical enquiry which is comparable, at his own level, with that undertaken by the professional historian. He is not merely collecting data which illustrates national themes, a false emphasis which is a perpetual temptation to the secondary history teacher with a syllabus to cover.

There is evidence that pupils are encouraged to work in this way (Murphy 1971). A project on family history with Murphy's top class at St Cuthbert's Junior School, Pemberton, near Wigan, included such activities as the construction of an imaginary family tree, the classification of types of evidence, and dealing with basic concepts – time, sequence, space, etc. In tackling the fundamental questions of 'How? Why? When?' the pupils were obviously working in a much more disciplined way than they would under the more traditional chalk and talk approach.

SIMULATIONS AND GAMES

In many ways the use of simulations and games represents a further extension of the use of sources and activity methods in the history classroom, as is illustrated by Nichol's chapter in Part II on history at the Priory School for Boys, Shrewsbury. They have gained a very firm foothold in the United States and all the signs indicate that, over the past five years, there has been a very rapid extension of their use in England. Milburn (1972) has suggested that simulations are now coming of age and their use will be one of the most important challenges facing history teachers in the future. Broadly speaking a distinction should be made between board games and simulations. The former are usually much more structured with clearly defined roles, and they are likely to be more popular with younger pupils. Simulations are much more complex in that they demand role-playing by the pupils and are much more open-ended in that in-dividual responses determine much more the direction in which movement takes place so that the eventual outcome cannot be predicted.

The advantages claimed for the use of simulation exercises are numerous. Rayner (1972) found that in the United States simulation was seen not so much as a game but as 'a practical demonstration of some academic concept which even experienced teachers had previously known only in the light of their intellect', while participation in a 'game' produced a depth of realism and a sense of involvement that had a great educational impact. Simulations are also held to lead to more cooperation and discussion between students and to encourage the teacher to become an adviser rather than a fountain of information, a role which is more acceptable to teachers who prefer inquiry methods. It is also claimed for simulations that the greater element of oral work involved enables the less able child to make a more positive contribution than would normally be the case. But some teachers do question the place of simulations. A fundamental criticism is that, if history is concerned with the establishment of the unique, simulation – which involves considerable generalisation – directly contradicts this. Further, it is questionable whether the use of simulations does lead to significant differences in learning retention, critical thinking or attitude, as compared to other approaches to history in the classroom (Milburn 1972). Milburn also indicates that simulations may be criticised for leading to a distortion of reality through their compression into the space of a few minutes of events which have taken years to unfold.

Much research will have to be carried out before there can be any firm conclusions about the real value of games and simulations. None the less, it is evident that their growing popularity does reflect the new attitude to the teaching of history. They call on a range of skills, including the location and analysis of sources, the communication of ideas, the taking into account of other people's viewpoints, and the making of decisions. They also demand considerable involvement on the part of the pupil and they therefore reflect general pedagogical development. At the same time games and simulations are only two of several approaches to history teaching which require the use of these techniques and they should be seen as complementing areas such as family history and demography, rather than competing with them.

DRAMA IN HISTORY TEACHING

Increasing evidence is available of the growth of the popularity of drama in history teaching, the best material being found in the work of Fines and Verrier (1974). An example of one approach to history through drama is contained in Part II in Verrier's description of a project at Clanfield County Primary School, Hampshire. The logic that underpins the use of drama in the classroom bears close resemblance to that claimed for simulation. It is intended that through drama children should develop their historical understanding, while at the same time gaining enjoyment and interest in their study. They gain that understanding both through acting out the parts of the characters they study, and through pursuing background research in order to set the scene for the play. In so doing they are required to be active, to locate and to use relevant sources, and to recreate the past as authentically as they can – tasks that are rigorous in their demands.

A good example of the above was the production of a play on Elizabeth England at the Abbey Junior School, Reading (Thornton 1971). There a class of top juniors, after studying the Elizabethan period, decided to produce a play. Real historical benefits were gained because the pupils had to conduct their own research in order to make the play as authentic as possible in terms of such aspects as language, dress and furnishings. Similarly Medlycott (1973) produced a historical play at Sutton Park School, County Dublin. After making a special study of the reign of Henry II a mixed-ability group of boys and girls built up a play on Henry II and Thomas à Becket. Medlycott considered the play a success because pupils proved capable of stepping inside the period and asking 'how' and 'why' as well as 'what'. Certainly the discussion that followed the performance of the play suggested that, although the pupils were young, they could defend their own parts and discuss church–state relations in the period in question. As with the Abbey Junior School the key to success seems to lie in the fact that the play came at the conclusion of research into the topic.

The use of drama must be regarded as one of several ways of developing the pupil's interest in history, and of introducing him to the methodology of the subject. More significantly, however, in addition to its use in stimulating enthusiasm and developing historical skills, drama may also be seen to play a major role in arousing the pupil's historical imagination, one of the most important but neglected aspects of historical study.

Conclusion

Important developments are evidently taking place in the classroom, although the pace of change is slow. Considerable attention is being paid to the shape and content of the syllabus as is reflected in the decline of the chronological outline of British or European history and in the increased attention paid to world and local history. At the same time there is a much greater emphasis on the process of historical study, as is evidenced by the popularity of the source method in its various guises. The developments in schools reflect, to a large extent, what is happening in the universities. The picture is a confused one, though, and important questions must be answered if a really coherent school history curriculum is to be devised. These questions relate particularly to the need to define the common elements and the distinctive qualities of the various areas of study – world history, demography, economic history, etc. – now found in universities. If the character of these can be established it will become much simpler to make decisions about the shape and content of the school syllabus and about the teaching strategies that should be employed in the classroom. At the present time history has an infinite variety of shapes and forms and the lack of precision in its definition makes it more difficult to defend its position in the school curriculum.

PART II

7 The History of Chief David: an approach to history through drama

R. L. Verrier

Bishop Otter College of Education, Chichester

This paper is a description of a unit of work carried out by a college of education history lecturer with a class of top primary pupils from Clanfield County Primary School, Hampshire. The work developed over one afternoon for each of six weeks, plus some follow-up by the class teacher. It was intended in the unit to explore the use of role-playing techniques as an economical tool for the teacher and pupils in their investigation of historical material, and to demonstrate that the study of history in school should relate more closely to the work of the professional historians.

During the first two weeks pupils spent some time recalling a series of events in the immediate past, in particular a visit to Portsmouth made seven weeks previously. Attention was focused on the different ways in which the past is recalled by individuals and it was decided to concentrate in the next few weeks upon the concept of 'significant' events in time.

As a starting point the pupils were asked to create a significant group event and this shared event in time would be used as a springboard for further developments. It was decided to 'create' an event in history rather than choose a real historical event because the writer wanted pupils to experience and live through the significant event internally rather than study an event from the outside.

The most effective way of creating from within was by employing role-playing methods. For this lesson pupils worked in the school hall. They sat in a circle and were asked to imagine they were living at a time when most people knew nothing about writing skills. This suggested for the pupils the idea of living long ago. 'At present we are sitting around a fire, each person is engaged in making something he will find useful for himself or for others.' Pupils started to mime activities and were told they might need to talk to one another about their activity. After several minutes the writer asked the pupils to explain *why* they were doing that particular job at the moment. The mimed activity showed clearly what was being done. As various pupils explained their activities two significant things happened:

1 Pupils developed their replies by accepting what previous speakers had said, and a group understanding began to develop. Gradually the whole group accepted a common group identity and belief.

2 Some answers pointed towards a significant event due to take place the following day.

From these replies everybody including the writer, who found himself taking up the role of visitor to the tribe, discovered that they were living in the early Iron Age and that the tribal leader had recently been killed while out hunting. Tomorrow a new leader would be chosen as a result of proving his physical skills, and then he would ritually be made leader. Finally the event would be marked by a feast. The visitor to the tribe then pointed out that probably many preparations had to be made and therefore he would let people get on with their different tasks. The pupils then created a ritual ceremony of leader-making and followed this by a feast. At the end of the afternoon the people of the tribe were asked how they thought they might mark this significant day in the history of their tribe. They started to explore the possibilities of paintings and oral accounts.

It is important to observe that the event these pupils chose to create is one in which a time of change is about to occur. The new leader may prove himself unworthy of real leadership, his tribe may enter a period of decline in which their enemies triumph over them so that they lose a distinct tribal identity. Alternatively the leader may initiate a period of glory and prosperity leading to conquest and 'empire' building. 'Change' is essentially what history is about. The

pupils' drama had led them directly into the start of a particular instance of change in the history of the tribe.

The next stage of development in the work presented a problem.
Change is a difficult thing to appreciate for people living through a
period of change. Essentially it requires the spectator role of
historian, or of one looking at change from a distance. The pupils had
enjoyed the drama. Could they now disengage from the participant
role of tribal people and take up the new spectator role of historians,
by looking at their created event from a distance?

The following week pupils were asked to imagine themselves as
present-day historians looking back through time at the tribe, and in
particular at its new leader. Pupils were asked if they thought the
new leader proved himself to be a great man who initiated a period of
fortune and success for his tribe or a weak and feckless man. All the
pupils decided on the former. The boy chosen for leader was popular
with the class. Pupils were then asked, as historians, to produce a
history book of the new leader. They discussed the type of material
the history book should contain and decided upon accounts of the
deeds of the leader which illustrated his 'good' character. This information, they decided, would be drawn from cave paintings, oral
traditions and archaeology. The finished book was to be called 'The
History of Chief David'. The work on the history book was com-
pleted during the following week. The class teacher's active participation proved particularly valuable at this stage and the pupils
were extremely proud of the finished professional-looking product.

The next stage of the work was dictated by two factors – the obvious pride of the pupils in their book, and the unanimous opinion of
'The Historians' about the good character of Chief David. The
professional historian is always interested when new sources of information come to light. He is also interested in reconsidering the
verdicts of previous historians dealing with his special areas of interest. It was therefore decided by the writer to challenge 'The
History of Chief David' by producing fresh evidence and an explanation of Chief David which contradicted the book. As documentary
evidence would not be available as a primary source, the nature of the
new evidence must be archaeological.

The new evidence was presented to the pupils in the form of photographs of finds uncovered below Chief David's palace. They included well-preserved skeletons of human bodies, the skulls of which were clearly damaged; a treasure hoard; and a piece of pottery of Chief David. Far from being a good man, David has murdered his enemies and buried them beneath his palace. The treasure hoard represented items taken from his people by a greedy, self-seeking leader. These findings and this explanation would invalidate the pupils' 'History of Chief David' unless they could explain the fresh archaeological evidence in a different way. The pupils then worked in groups on the fresh evidence and finally offered the following explanations:

These skeletons were of Chief David's warriors who all died in battle in similar fashion. Honoured dead of Chief David's tribe are always buried under the Palace in order to be near the living leader of their tribe.

These skeletons belonged to witches who were ceremonially killed by removing the brain and firmly buried under the stone floor of the Palace.

The hoard of valuables belonging to the leader was hidden for safety in time of war or trouble. The Palace was obviously the safest and best defended place for security.

In the light of these statements the visiting historian decided to think again about his own explanation of the evidence!

In the course of their work so far, pupils had been challenged to behave and think in a manner that is analogous to that of the historian. The role play about the tribe and the subsequent writing of 'The History of Chief David' were vital to the belief and involvement of the pupils in the work that followed. They had created an object – the book – to defend, and this defence was carried out in the same mode as that used by a professional historian when defending his historical position. The range of language activities involved in this work is probably obvious to the reader. Discussion, debate, small group social language, role play and imaginative written work formed the types of language situation encountered by the pupils. Research work in the usual sense was not involved and for the next lesson it was decided that pupils should become involved in the close scrutiny of written language, using 'The History of Chief David' as a source.

The writer started the next session by welcoming 'members of the Historical Association' to the annual meeting at which a 'visiting professor' was introduced (the head of the college of education history department) who chose to use this visit as a time to challenge two of the stories in the book about Chief David. During the ensuing lesson the Clanfield historians had to defend their book against the accusation of exaggeration. In the course of the lesson they showed the 'professor', through a series of role play presentations, exactly how things had happened to Chief David. The two episodes in the book that the professor had attacked did indeed take place as described. This description probably does not do full justice to the pupils, who took a fragment of written history and brought life and meaning and interpretation into it.

For the final week of this unit pupils were presented with a few badly damaged written documents produced after Chief David's death. By the time these documents came into existence people had learnt to write. The documents were incomplete but they could suggest that Chief David's death was a welcome relief for his people. Could it be interpreted in any other way? This was the final challenge for the historians of Chief David. It involved another area of language study in which the focus was upon written words and the significance of words. Again it represents an aspect of the historian's work.

What has emerged as significant about this unit of work briefly described in this paper? As far as the writer is concerned these seem to be the main points.

To attempt to describe this unit of work as 'history' in the conventional sense of school history is to try to put a quart in a pint pot, since the work also covered areas of language development and drama. Pupils have experienced, for example, a range of language activities in both participant and spectator role and these have been explored mainly in oral form. 'The History of Chief David' is the main written form. However the last two lessons involved an examination of written language in order to discover meaning within a context and also the connection between real experience and its transformation into a symbolic form. The book represents a movement from vicarious and real experience into symbols. The study of written documents, described in the last two lessons, represents a move from the brief, concise, packed symbol back into real experience or life in action.

If we wish to use labels like 'history' then we must recognise the true breadth of the term as understood and practised by the professional historian. His history and the school subject 'history' as it appears on the curriculum should be of the same nature and quality. The project on Chief David showed that it is possible for pupils to engage in an activity parallel and similar in nature and philosophy to that followed by professional historians. The difference lies not in the nature of the activity, but in the degree of abstraction possible for pupils. The activity of pupils must be developed in concrete terms that pupils can see and handle. The principal tool for achieving this level of activity in the work described was through role play methods. The ceremony of Chief David was active group role play, but throughout the rest of the work pupils were identifying with the attitudes of historians – they were taking up the role of historians. The writer of this paper took up a role as well. Without the role-playing tool it would be impossible to experience this sort of historical experience from inside and the implicit belief of this paper is that pupils need to experience history 'from inside'.

8 History games and simulations

J. Nichol
Priory School for Boys, Shrewsbury

Over the past five years I have incorporated a wide range of history games and simulations into my history courses for the eleven- to eighteen-year age range. The games have been designed in response to my attitudes towards history teaching, and the classroom situation which has faced me in three schools. The latter factor has been crucial, and the games have had to be practical in relation to both timetabling in a secondary school and the overall educational goals of the school. Although I would have liked to have incorporated a much greater range of simulations into our upper-school work, the problem of restricted time with examination forms has limited the opportunities.

History simulations are based on the simple idea that pupils should act out the role or roles of characters in history. As such, it is a rationalisation of much previous classroom practice. But, as a rationalisation, it enables the techniques to be much more systematically developed and applied. Emphasis needs to be placed upon it as a teaching technique. It is designed to be used alongside other methods such as fieldwork, workcards and drama. It is in no way designed to supersede existing methods of teaching. Indeed, it is intended to be an auxiliary called in to the aid of the hard-pressed classroom teacher. However, it will be suggested that simulation can function as a central 'spine' or theme to a course of study. As such, it has been successfully used in the mixed-ability situation, and served as a common point of reference for mixed-ability groups.

When pupils take on the roles of characters in history they can do this in three distinct ways: as individual characters, as members of a small group or as members of larger bodies. Correspondingly this results in single, group or class role play exercises. As a single character the pupil can take the part of a figure such as an ironmaster during the Industrial Revolution; as a member of a small group he might be a delegate at a conference, such as the Congress of Vienna where he might represent either Metternich, Talleyrand, Castlereagh or Alexander I; or in a class role play he could be a member of a shipload of colonists establishing a colony in North America in the early seventeenth century. Whatever the type of simulation exercise, the pupil plays out his role against as accurate a historical framework as possible. The framework thus attempts to mirror the historical reality at a given point in time. By taking decisions upon information contained within the framework or subsequently supplied, the pupils give the framework a dynamic aspect. This enables them to grasp some of the multiplicity of possible outcomes which might have occurred in any historical situation.

Because of my desire to make the historical framework, and the information fed to the pupils, as accurate as possible, I increasingly base simulations upon resource material. The topology on p. 71 shows the integration of history games and simulations into a resource-based approach to history teaching, and how simulation is one of a range of teaching techniques related to an overall programme of educational aims and skills. This programme is shown in the first column. The second column deals with the materials and resources available for use with classes. The third column covers the chronology and historical framework against which the evidence and resources have meaning. The final column indicates the different teaching techniques available with the resources. The distinctions are only intended as a rough guide, and there is a wide overlap between the different categories. History simulation can be seen as an aggregate activity, drawing upon the whole range of resources available.

Within the categories of single, group or class role play exercises we employ a wide range of simulation activity. This covers board

History teaching and simulations in history

Educational aims and skills	Evidence/ resources	Chronology and framework	Teaching techniques
Vocabulary Reference skills Memory Comprehension Translation Analysis Imagination Synthesis Judgement Evaluation Communication	1 The teacher The class	The facts of history Chronology Historical framework	1 Dictation, chalk and talk exposition
	2 Documentary – Printed – Manuscript (Primary) (Secondary)		2 Note-taking Worksheet Workcard Resource units Reading Models
	3 Remains – Artefacts – Structures – Archaeology		3 Local history Archaeology Models
	4 Visuals – Paintings – Drawings – Photos – Film – Videotape – Prints		4 Workcard Resource units Picture analysis Slides Filmstrip Film Video
	5 Speech – Audio – Tapes – Memory		5 Tapes Interviews Drama Debates Discussion
	6 Traces – Statistics		6 Worksheets
	7 Composite sources		7 Essays Projects Games and simulations

games; map games in which pupils may choose sites, 'fill in' a blank map progressively, or fill in a map according to a predetermined outline; and discussion games involving either class debates or intergroup negotiations. Each of these simple role play exercises can exist independently of the others. A number of different simulation exercises can be combined into complex games, such as the Roman settlement game described below. In preparing games for the classroom there is a danger of trying to write complex games which are in·fact a number of related simulations.

An examination of some simulations at present in use demonstrates how they are developed and implemented. They are slotted into the teaching programme at an apposite moment, and are *consciously* designed to complement our existing teaching programme. In writing our simulations we follow the outlines for the different kinds of simulations as laid down in the Longman series of history games, published at York (Longman Group 1973). In the second year (twelve to thirteen age range) we employ a simulation on Roman settlement, part of which is shown below. The simulation is complex, and is made up of three simple games: a single-role-play map game, involving site choice; a single-role-play map game, involving progressive development of an outline map; and a class debate. The first part involves the choice of a site for a Roman camp and town, and is based on the topography of Roman Shropshire. Already care has been taken to make the simulation as historically accurate as possible.

Part 2 deals with the building of a Roman camp upon the site chosen. The pupil represents an adviser to the Roman general Scapula, who conquered the region. The simulation uses an outline map (figure 8.1) of the site of Wroxeter, a Roman town in Shropshire, and a simple framework of rules:

Having selected the site, the next task is to build the camp. For warfare in Wales you need one legion – about 6,000 men, who will be permanently based in the new camp. You must choose exactly where on the site, shown on Map 2 [figure 8.1], the best spot for the camp will be.

The camp will be square or rectangular, as these are easiest to defend. The walls will be between 300 to 400 metres long. It will be built as small as

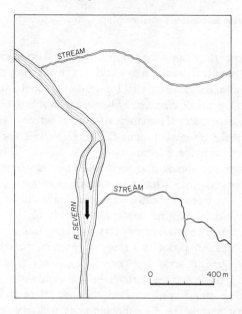

Figure 8.1 *Map of the site of Wroxeter*

possible, with no wasted space, so that fewer men will be needed to guard it.

Inside the plan the buildings must be laid out as efficiently as possible, based on a grid street pattern. The camp will contain the following features:

  1 A defensive wall and gateways
  2 A water supply
  3 Barracks for the men
  4 A building for the legion's headquarters
  5 A house for the commander
  6 Quarters for the other officers
  7 A cookhouse
  8 Toilets
  9 Stables for the cavalry (about 200 horses)
10 An armoury
11 A granary
12 Quartermaster's stores
13 Workshops

Draw in these features in pencil on Map 2, on a spot you have chosen for the camp.

To construct their camp the pupils use original evidence concerning Roman camps. In addition to a wide range of books, pamphlets, resource units and slides they visit local museums containing Roman remains and the site of Wroxeter. They are thus able to tie in a wide range of resource material into their simulation activity. The simulation was written by my colleague S. N. E. G. Newell, and has been used with a wide range of forms.

Increasingly our simulations such as 'Roman settlement' have a simple framework into which we can tie resources, particularly documents, which are duplicated on either a Banda or Roneo. Often these are the only resource material available to the peripatetic history teacher, who moves from class to class. Although we have regarded simulation as one of a range of teaching methods, we are working on a game to serve as a 'core' for a course on the industrial, agrarian and transport revolutions in the eighteenth–nineteenth centuries. The simulation is based on a series of local studies, covering East Shropshire. A local community will serve as the focal point, and the pupils will simulate the reaction of the inhabitants to the coming of the turnpike, canals and railways, enclosure and agricultural change, and industrialisation.

What is the benefit of our simulations? The most important is that it introduces a major element of stimulus into a course, and provides motivation in history. In particular it develops educational skills concerned with comprehension, translation, empathy, analysis, imagination and communication. It introduces a major element of verbal communication into the classroom, and with pupils often working closely together it definitely helps to break down barriers within the classroom. Certainly it has helped to make the study of history a lively and meaningful experience for the students involved.

9 A mixed mode O level examination in history at the Graham Balfour High School, Stafford

D. G. Kirby and S. Roberts

We first learned of the mixed mode history examination in 1973 through R. A. Lewis, the Staffordshire County Advisory Officer for history. In 1974 we were admitted to the limited number of schools which are permitted by the J.M.B. to do a mixed mode examination and first began to teach the course in September of that year. Our pupils will not therefore be entered for the examination until next summer and so, as yet, our experience of teaching and examining a mixed mode O level is incomplete. Even so, it has proved rewarding, and worthwhile lessons have been learned.

Our decision to develop a mixed mode course arose from discontent with the restrictions imposed by Mode I O level courses. Experience with the traditional history syllabuses, and the methods of examining them, led to the conclusion that they were not fully satisfactory. There are a number of reasons for this. The typical O level syllabus covers one historical period but neither requires nor encourages depth of knowledge and understanding in any area, however educationally sound such specialisation might be. Although the final examination gives considerable choice of questions and therefore allows some selection of material by the teacher, all areas are examined at equal depth. No real scope is given for the pupil to make a concentrated study of any one area of the syllabus. Despite the teacher's freedom to select from within the syllabus it is difficult for him to justify in-depth treatment of a part of the syllabus, particularly if he knows that this part will probably receive scant attention in the final examination.

Similar restrictions operate in the choice of skills which the teacher intends to develop in his pupils. The final examination in a Mode I O level takes the form of short essay-type answers. The skills being tested in this manner are primarily recall, the ability to organise information into a coherent whole and the ability to communicate under pressure in essay form. All of these are important but they are by no means the only historical skills. Others, of equal importance, are not tested at all. This has considerable implications for the type of teaching that takes place in the classroom and for the materials used in teaching. Too much emphasis is given to the use of the classbook or to books that give brief coverage of a period, to the making of notes and to the practice of essay writing. The most conscientious teacher finds little encouragement for the use of a wider choice of materials or for the development of other skills.

The aims in formulating a mixed mode O level course were therefore to continue the teaching of those skills already developed by the Mode I course but also to allow for the development and examination of a further range of historical skills. Only by the restriction of the factual content of the course could time be gained for the teaching of skills such as research techniques, comprehension, analysis, evaluation and synthesis. The use of documentary material of various types allows for the positive development of analysis and evaluation. Such material demands a critical approach through which the pupil will learn to separate pieces of information, identify inconsistency and recognise bias. Evaluation and correlation of information requires the assessment of relevance and of relative importance and, implicitly, of the formation of criteria to do this.

One of the major criticisms of the study of history under Mode I was that it allowed little time for specialisation by the pupil. The undertaking by the pupil of a piece of personal research is therefore another aim of the course. Such work necessitates the pupil's working with guidance but without a framework of information from the teacher. Under these circumstances reference and research skills must be mastered, including the ability to read widely, to comprehend, and to develop historical judgement. Thus the pupil must organise his own material and present a coherent piece of work, necessitating the use of skills of communication and presentation. The use of project work also allows for the development of an awareness of local history illustrative of the national situation.

The syllabus is essentially the J.M.B. syllabus G, Europe and the Modern World 1870 to the Present Day, which covers a wide variety of topics, national and international, during the last hundred years. The normal procedure is for pupils to answer five essay-type questions in two and a half hours. The mixed mode arrangement with the J.M.B. permits this to be considerably modified. Mixed mode pupils take the same paper as all other pupils but answer only three questions for which one and three-quarter hours are allowed. They are not allowed to answer questions from Section 1 of the examination paper, which consists of 'Four questions ranging over the whole period requiring several short answers'. The answer papers are marked and dealt with in the same way as are the longer two and a half hour ones, but they carry 60 per cent of the marks. The remaining 40 per cent of the marks is awarded by the school. Our school has been authorised to award 25 per cent for a project and 15 per cent for an internally set documents paper, although it is possible to negotiate other types of examination with a different balance of marks.

The reduction of emphasis on the essay paper enables the number of topics to be studied for this purpose to be reduced. The reduced syllabus had to be agreed with the board which is concerned to ensure that the course is not too truncated and that pupils will still have an adequate choice of questions on the examination paper. In our case we chose to study the national histories of Great Britain and Germany throughout the period and of Italy, Russia and the U.S.A. in the twentieth century. In addition we deal fully with a number of international topics, the First and Second World Wars, their causes and consequences, international relations between the wars, the League of Nations, UNO and Europe since 1945.

A second element in the process of examining is the documents paper. Schools have for some time set their own documents papers under this scheme. As far as we are aware they have always been of the single extract type, similar in style to the ones set occasionally in

Section 1 of the Mode I paper. Our paper is rather different. We hope to test the ability to assess and correlate several pieces of information of different sorts from different sources. There is not space to print an example in full but one such paper dealing with the First World War presents the pupil with the following:

A A recruiting poster.
B General Haig's 'Special Order of the Day' 11th April, 1918.
C A letter to the press, 'A Mother's Answer to "A Common Soldier".'
D Extracts from the diary of Stephen Jenkyns.
E Three poems of Siegfried Sassoon, 'France', 'Suicide in the Trenches', and 'Blighter's'.
F An artist's impression of war on the Western Front 'The Harvest of Battle' by C. R. W. Nevinson.

The pupils are required to answer the following questions:

1 (a) With reference to the extracts C, D and E describe the attitudes to the war of those people who had not experienced it at first hand.
  (b) Estimate how much support that attitude had in England.
2 (a) With reference to the extracts D and E describe the attitudes of Sassoon and Jenkyns after they experienced the war.
  (b) Compare the attitudes described in 2 (a) with those of Jenkyns and Sassoon before they had experienced the war.
  (c) Compare the attitudes described in 2 (a) with those of Sir Douglas Haig.
3 Which picture, extract A or extract F, is a more accurate reflection of the conditions of fighting in the First World War? Use the documentary evidence of extracts D and E to justify your answer.

The third element is the project through which it is our intention to test the ability to write from, and to make extensive use of, primary sources. In order to minimise the external advantages enjoyed by individual pupils – such as a home life conducive to study, or money to spend on visits, books or pictures – and to ensure as fair a test of ability as may be, we have carefully limited the topics from which a project may be chosen, and we have supplied a full range of secondary and primary sources from which the projects are largely written. The topics are all of British social history in the nineteenth and twentieth centuries. We have been fortunate in having available for our pupils' use a series of primary source booklets prepared by R. A. Lewis, which are intended for project use. Being local in origin and illustrating local history, they have encouraged pupils to follow up their classroom work with visits to the County Record Office and to local sites. One major problem in tackling project work in this way was cost, and we are very glad to acknowledge the financial help that R. A. Lewis made available to us.

In writing their projects pupils are permitted class time equivalent to the marks carried by the work, in our case 25 per cent, and are subject to very close guidance and control. Our purpose is to teach the skills involved and we do not assume that they are to be acquired other than by our teaching.

In opting for a mixed mode examination we do not particularly expect or hope to alter the order of merit of pupils, or significantly to affect the pass rate. Our experience to date is insufficient, as we made clear at the beginning of this essay, for us to draw any firm conclusions, but the board's examiners maintain that the order of merit produced by the essay examination is not substantially different from that produced by other modes of examining. Be that as it may, we have already felt and seen advantages from the mixed mode. It would not be fair to say that it makes lighter work for either teacher or pupil. Indeed, in so far as the teacher is concerned, there is a great deal of additional, unpaid work in preparing examinations and in marking and moderating both them and the projects. But teaching is changed. It can be more varied and relaxed. It is possible to give over a greater proportion of classroom time to private reading and, through that, to encourage the development of a more mature attitude to work and to historical problems. Although some pupils are not very keen on this type of work, and find parts of their project work tedious, the overall reaction is favourable. There is far less emphasis on learning facts by heart and the experience of research is generally accepted as a rewarding one which has generated a real enthusiasm for and interest in the topic work.

Perhaps the greatest tangible gain has been in the pupils' increasing awareness that history is not primarily about facts in a concrete, immutable sense, but about judgements, and judgements which are usually based on less than complete evidence. We also believe, though our experience is too recent for us to be dogmatic, that the course is a better preparation for A level work than the more traditional O level examination course and that pupils will be enabled to make the transition from the fifth to the sixth form more easily.

10 A C.S.E. Mode III based on continuous assessment at Clough Hall Comprehensive School, Kidsgrove

B. White

In the autumn term of 1970 a group of six North Staffordshire schools – of which Clough Hall Comprehensive was one – agreed to participate in running a joint Mode III C.S.E. scheme based on a common syllabus and method of assessment. The group adopted a social and economic history syllabus, designed by L. Breeze of Moorside Comprehensive School, which was similar in outline to sections of Syllabus B of the West Midlands Examination Board. It did differ in two important aspects, however, in that it involved a large element of local history and also allowed for a much more detailed study of selected topics.

The broad aim of the syllabus was 'to highlight the interrelationship between the historical development of North Staffordshire and that of the country as a whole, since about 1700'. It was also intended to afford a wider opportunity to use primary source material and make excursions into the field. This arose from the belief that, in using local source material to highlight national developments, not only would the work appear to be more relevant to the pupils, but pupils would also be encouraged to develop historical skills, as they would be working more in the style of the professional historian. Such goals are difficult to achieve, especially under a Mode I system where the majority of the marks are awarded for factual recall. We have therefore endeavoured to create learning situations in which pupils use historical skills other than mere factual recall and to ensure that pupils are fully rewarded for their use of those historical skills. We have also encouraged pupils of all abilities to work together and allowed them to work at their own pace within a broad time scale.

The syllabus is divided into six sections: Industrial Developments; Agricultural Development; Transport; Life and Health; Education, Working and Governing; and any local social or economic development not specifically mentioned in the rest of the syllabus. Each section is further divided into subsections, for example subsection B of Transport is 'Canals: The need for canals, particularly in N. Staffordshire; the canal engineers; the development of the canal network; the benefits of canals to midland industry; the decline of canals, and canals today'. The method of assessment was decided on only after considerable debate. The circular letter inviting the schools to participate in the scheme had suggested 25 per cent for the special study as in Mode I, 25 per cent for factual recall by means of objective questions, and 50 per cent for either three essay- or paragraph-type questions or on the basis of continuous assessment. We came down in favour of continuous assessment because we wanted our assessment to be based on our pupils' work over a period, rather than just on their performance on a given day. We also considered continuous assessment a better means of assessing the wider range of skills we hoped our pupils would acquire while, at the very least, we knew it would produce evidence of the normal work of our pupils under everyday conditions by eliminating the stress conditions of the examination room. We also hoped that the knowledge that all the marks awarded would contribute to their final assessment would encourage our pupils to work consistently over the whole period of the course.

We decided also that over a period of five terms, allowing one term for the special study, eight subsections of the syllabus would be studied, i.e. one from each section one to five and then any three others. Each pupil would be given an assignment (a scheme of work) on each subsection studied, the assignment involving approximately half a term's work. Each assignment would then be assessed by the pupil's teacher using the following criteria: the selection of relevant facts from a variety of sources – 20 per cent; interpretation of the relevant facts as shown by their use to argue effectively, criticise and analyse and illustrate and explain relationships – 15 per cent; presentation (layout) – 5 per cent; general impression, effort and initiative, a reserve for special credit – 10 per cent.

This scheme was one of the first Mode III schemes involving a large element of continuous assessment to be presented to the History Panel of the W.M.E.B. Initially the panel was very reluctant to accept a scheme involving such a large element of continuous assessment and such a small element of formal examination (and that consisting of objective questions). The panel also expressed concern about the weighting of the syllabus towards local history. However, after meeting the teachers from the participating schools and R.A. Lewis the History Adviser for Staffordshire, the panel accepted the scheme and quickly produced *Continuous Assessment: Notes for Guidance of History Teachers* which was based on the arguments put forward by our group at the meeting with the History Panel.

Regular meetings of the teachers involved were seen as essential from the start. These take place on average once a month, during school time, for the purpose of moderation of assignments, the writing and standardising of worksheets, for the selection of objective questions, and for general discussion of the course and regular revision of its objectives. At an early stage it became evident that eight assignments assessed on all the criteria listed above was not as valid a means of assessment as we had hoped. Because we found assignments tended to assess mainly the ability 'to select and collect relevant facts from a variety of sources', we changed the method of assessment to six assignments aimed at testing all the criteria, and two extended essays designed to test the pupils' comprehension (grasp) of relevant facts as shown by (a) interpretation and (b) the ability to argue effectively, to criticise and analyse from given data and to illustrate and explain historical relationships. Testing memory recall by using objective questions had also proved extremely difficult in the small group situation and so, instead of setting forty objective questions at the end of the course, we resolved to set twenty short-answer questions immediately after the completion of an assignment. At the present time the group is still struggling to find a means of testing, in a reliable and valid way, the historical skills and abilities involved in comprehension at all its levels.

The approach to an assignment is basically that of a historian. The pupils are encouraged to read around a subject and then to relate their reading to specific tasks as they occur on a worksheet. The tasks are so ordered as to demand the use of historical skills such as obtaining and checking information from both primary and secondary sources, and testing simple and more advanced comprehension of material. In its simplest form pupils are required to describe the relevant salient features of a piece of evidence, or to give the gist of the material read. At a higher level it demands the ability to formulate what is interesting or questionable about a piece of evidence or secondary source material. From this the skill of extrapolation is a natural step, as is the ability to evaluate evidence and make judgements on it.

The course also places a premium on literacy, since history is a highly literary subject, and it is very important to demand high standards of English at all times. Such insistence helps in the development of the basic skill of comprehension.

We are very fortunate in Staffordshire in so far as the availability of primary source material is concerned on account of the work of R. A. Lewis, who has been very active in producing books of source material on a variety of subjects. The worksheets used by the pupils lean heavily on these source books, but basic social and economic history textbooks, and books on specific topics, are also listed for reference. The worksheets have been produced by the individual schools and vetted by the teachers from the other participating schools.

Typical of the worksheets is the one on canals. Pupils are instructed to read through the worksheet carefully before starting work and reminded that credit will be given for illustrations, maps, sketches, diagrams, newspaper cuttings, etc., and, in particular, that they must make as much use as possible of the relevant source book – *Staffordshire Waterways*. They are then required to answer briefly two general questions – 'Why were canals built in this country in the eighteenth and nineteenth centuries?' and 'Who were the people who put up the money to build them?'. They are instructed that, in order to answer the two questions, they must consider the ways in which goods were transported before the canals were built, the changes that took place which meant that transport had to be made more efficient, and the sort of people who would be particularly interested in improving transport facilities.

In the next stage the pupils are asked to investigate the development of canals in Staffordshire. They look, for example, at the following questions – 'how were raw materials and finished products transported to and from the Potteries at the beginning of the eighteenth century?'; 'how were goods transported to and from other industrial towns in Staffordshire?'; 'were the Staffordshire iron masters and mine owners satisfied with the transport facilities available to them?'; 'why was Staffordshire in a particularly difficult position as far as transport was concerned?'; 'what people were particularly interested in getting canals built in Staffordshire?'; 'what did they have to do before they could start to build a canal?'; 'what canals were built in Staffordshire, and when?' and so on. The pupils are referred to the relevant documents to help them find the answers and the assignment continues in this way – by question and reference – so that a complete picture of canals in Staffordshire and their influence on, and place in, the national network is gradually built up.

A worksheet on a particular topic can be common to all the participating schools or it may be modified to allow for the different localities of the individual schools; a worksheet on education, for example, will have questions requiring examination of school logbooks in the area of the particular school rather than in North Staffordshire at large. This partial standardisation of worksheets allows for more reliable and valid assessment of the pupil's work. Each assignment is first marked by the pupil's teacher and then is moderated by teachers from the participating schools. In effect, there are eight moderation meetings and a final awards meeting. Owing to the numbers involved it is not possible to moderate every piece of work of every pupil, but during the course each pupil has at least two pieces of work moderated. For the awarding of the grade the mark for the worst assignment is ignored and the pupils' marks for the other seven are averaged. This mark is then added to the special study mark (moderated by the board) and the standardised objective test mark (now short-answer questions), giving a final total out of 100. The awards meeting is attended by two representatives of the W.M.E.B. History Panel who receive the recommendations of the group and examine samples of pupils' work around the cut-off points for each grade. At the monthly moderation meetings standards are kept firmly in mind. Thus the main task at the awards meeting is that of deciding exact cut-off points. To date the board's moderators have accepted the group's recommendations and have remarked on the high standard of the work presented.

Although critics of continuous assessment suggest a tendency for internally awarded marks to result in bunching towards the top end of the scale, we have been able to produce a good spread of marks and have awarded grades throughout the full C.S.E. range. Teacher assessment we feel has been made more reliable, consistent, and sufficiently objective by having it regularly moderated by other teachers. This regular moderation of each other's pupils has also helped considerably to improve the ability of individual teachers to describe the attainment of their own pupils in terms of marks comparable with those awarded by their colleagues in participating schools.

We have found some disadvantages in using continuous assessment. The planning and carrying out of the assessment does involve the teacher in a great deal of extra work, but in the end this is worthwhile because it does allow for a much closer examination of what is being taught. We have also found that continuous assessment does not suit all pupils. Some of the weaker candidates have become discouraged, not so much by a succession of low marks as by the fact that they have not been prepared to make a consistent effort. It has not been our experience however that 'late developers' have been unduly penalised for inferior performance in the early part of the course. Excluding the worst assignment from the average of marks has allowed pupils to have at least one 'off period'. Further, as the continuous assessment carries only 50 per cent of the marks, pupils can raise their final percentage mark by means of the special study and factual recall tests.

Overall we have certainly benefited from our experience in teaching the course and working with the other schools involved. The regular meetings of the history teachers concerned has resulted in a constant interchange of ideas and questioning of objectives, while also affording a regular opportunity to see other people's work. In addition there is the knowledge for our pupils that they will receive a grade for the work they are doing regularly in the classroom situation and that any improvement in their work can only improve the final grade awarded. Since the work begins in the immediate locality and spreads outwards, it is also immediately more tangible and more easily comprehended. There is the added interest that the primary source material concerns places and names known to the pupils. One can only hope that ultimately the historical skills and abilities that are being developed will be applied by our pupils to the contemporary scene, and that this approach will have created, if not budding historians, then at least a genuine interest in the past – particularly that of the local area.

11 History in a scheme of integrated studies at Sidney Stringer School and Community College, Coventry

V. Mason

Team teaching in integrated studies demands much hard work from the contributing members. They have to overcome the organisational difficulties involved while at the same time ensuring that approaches to their own subject do have academic respectability. The study of the theme 'industry and cities', for example, obviously has considerable scope for historical analysis, but this could easily be lost sight of or misused without a full understanding of the issues involved and a willingness to be adaptable and work hard. There are, however, real benefits to be gained. In working in a team the historian has a good opportunity to inform his fellow members of his own individual approach, while at the same time benefiting from the varying insights of the others. The result for the classroom can be very healthy and history can certainly benefit as a subject.

One of the key problems in implementing integrated studies programmes is that most teachers involved have received little or no training in the skills required in team teaching. In this context our experience at Sidney Stringer may prove helpful to the history teacher planning to become involved in an integrated studies team. We work on the basis of a House of 100–120 pupils and four teachers. We do have the advantage of a timetabled team meeting of one lesson a week for each team of teachers and it would be very difficult indeed to plan effectively without such regular meetings. Various patterns of team planning have been used but the one that seems to work best is as follows. The team meets to discuss the outlines of the next term's work. They have to consider not only their own inclinations but also the general balance of the unit, the covering of certain skills over the whole year, and the resource materials that have already been made. Once the team has decided on the outline of the term's work, responsibility is assigned for different areas — providing resources, doing lead lessons, booking films and equipment or doing whatever is necessary for the planned work to take place. If this involves the making of new resource material then that material has to be available for prior inspection (i.e. before it is printed) by the other team members.

As you can imagine this level of team work imposes heavy demands on the individuals concerned. Teachers are being asked to expose their weaknesses and frailties in a way that would not be necessary if they could shut themselves in a classroom with thirty children. The following are a few guidelines to facilitate teamwork:

1 Rank should mean nothing in a team. A faculty head cannot use his superior status to avoid fair criticism. A new member of staff has just as much right to express criticisms and wishes as anyone else and discussion should centre on what is being said and suggested, not on who says it. If the team cannot agree, the team leader may have to take a decision simply because of time deadlines. In my school the team leader is not necessarily the most senior teacher present in the team, a fact that helps formally to cancel out school ranks like 'faculty head'.

2 Everyone is going to submit ideas for inspection and so, on the principle that it is your turn next, criticism and suggestion must be given tactfully and in a positive, as opposed to destructive, form. The team leader is responsible for ensuring that this is the tone that predominates in meetings.

3 When a teacher submits new resources the material is always presented 'in rough' — not typed ready for going to the printing room. This is a good defensive ploy since the teachers do not feel that their reputation is staked on the work submitted — they are showing an

acceptance of their own fallibility and a willingness to change and accept criticism. In addition, the fact that four minds have considered the materials reduces the danger of glaring errors, while at the same time ensuring that, because the materials are less of an individual's resource, they are more likely to be usable by another team – an important economic consideration.

The historian working in an integrated studies team has considerable responsibility as he must ensure that the integrity of his subject is maintained. He should be particularly concerned to see that the following concepts and skills are developed within the integrated programme. It is fundamental that the pupils should acquire an understanding of the idea of change over time, and that they should gain a concept of the time framework. Efforts should be made to ensure that they develop the ability to collect information from a wide variety of sources and that they should be able to piece together information so collected in order to produce a coherent picture of the subject being studied. Certainly the historian should dispel the image that studying history means learning, parrot-fashion, masses of facts about any given period.

The integrated studies course at Sidney Stringer occupies a substantial part of the pupil's time during the first three years in school. Teaching is done within faculties, and integrated studies – of which history is a part – comes under the faculty of humanities. The timetable is so designed that six periods are devoted to integrated studies and these may occupy one and a half mornings or two afternoons a week. The work is approached on a thematic basis, the various humanities subject areas contributing to the study of the themes. In the fourth and fifth years all pupils do the school's own C.S.E. Mode III continuous assessment course in social studies and they also have the opportunity to select history, geography and R.E. as exam options. Thus the foundations laid during the integrated studies course of the first three years form an important basis for work in years four and five.

To show how some of the ideas outlined above can be applied I would like to describe one theme studied in the third-year integrated inquiries course at Sidney Stringer. It is called 'industries and cities'. The theme lays a good foundation for a new unit on the Third World which has been introduced into the social studies C.S.E. course. 'Industries and cities' was tackled in four units:

1 Reading O.S. maps – since O.S. maps are a specialist way of telling us about how any particular area of land is utilised by man.

2 The production of food – connection between terrain, soil, climate and the food that can be produced in a certain area.

3 Industrialisation – what it means; industrialisation of Britain; the meaning of technology and the existence of different levels of technology; what it is like to live in an industrialised society; the distribution of wealth – how people can become rich, what poverty means.

4 The Third World (i.e. non-industrialised) – what is it? What are its characteristics, the relationship between the industrialised world and the Third World; especially in trade and aid.

Within a theme such as this, with its obvious geographical applications, the problem for a historian is to ensure that the historical applications are also made explicit. In Unit 1, for example, it is possible to familiarise the pupils with evidence of earlier settlements and some earlier land uses. In Unit 2 there is opportunity for a historical study of the development of British agriculture although this was not, in fact, an opportunity that was utilised, simply through lack of time. Unit 3, of course, lends itself very well to the use of historical perspectives. We tried to stress the fact that industrialisation is a process that has happened in different places at different times and that industrialisation is not itself a static thing as a country can have a second wave of industrialisation. The following worksheet shows one way in which this theme was approached.

Bradford and Coventry

Bradford and Coventry are two English industrial towns. They were not industrialised and did not grow at the same time.

Here are their population figures (in thousands)

Bradford	1801	13	1851	104	1901	280
	1811	16	1861	106	1911	288
	1821	26	1871	146	1921	286
	1831	44	1881	183	1931	298
	1841	67	1891	216	1951	292
Coventry	1801	16	1851	36	1901	70
	1811	18	1861	41	1911	106
	1821	21	1871	38	1921	128
	1831	27	1881	42	1931	167
	1841	31	1891	53	1951	258

1 Use these facts to draw a bar graph showing the growth of Bradford and Coventry.
2 *Answer these questions*
   (a) When was Bradford growing at its fastest?
   (b) When was Coventry growing at its fastest?

The pupils were then required to pursue their own independent, library-based research in order to establish the nature of the industries associated with the two towns so that they could come to a fuller understanding of the varying aspects of industrialisation. Other activities in this unit included an analysis of the plough as an example of a piece of technology – to see how it had changed and what these changes meant for the society that used it – and using slides to establish points of difference between life in an industrialised and non-industrialised society. (The pupils were then asked to explore these aspects of life in their own industrialised society – for example the separation of home and work and dependence on a money wage.)

The biggest problem proved to be the actual size of the theme when based on these four units. It was planned that the study of the theme would last a term, but even the long Christmas term proved too short. Lack of time is invariably a problem but the teacher can help himself. In order to be economic in his use of the time available, for example, one question that the teacher needs constantly to ask about the work he is preparing is: 'Is this an entirely new concept or skill that I am introducing or is it a variation on one I have already planned in this unit?' If the latter then it may form an option rather than part of the core work that all pupils must do. Thus, in the work on the industrialisation of Britain, the period of Britain's industrialisation and the coming of new industries was established in the core work, whereas the study of the coal, pottery and iron and steel industries formed options and not three compulsory areas of study for all pupils.

I do not wish to claim that this scheme of work is perfected or highly polished. It has proved of worth, however, in that it does call on a range of important historical skills and concepts. I think, for example, that the concept of change has been well established, but that the 'why' of change needs to be developed. There has also been good scope for the use of various research skills and for practice in the evaluation of different forms of evidence. Thus, even though history is not the core subject, in studying the theme 'industries and cities' the pupils have gained some insight into the nature of historical study.

12 Schools Council projects on history teaching: a wider perspective

D. W. James
Madeley College of Education

Indicative of the current interest in the state of history teaching in schools is the following list of relevant Schools Council projects: Environmental Studies 5–13; History, Geography and Social Science 8–13 (the materials of which are published under the title *Place, Time and Society*); Integrated Studies; Humanities Curriculum Project; History 13–16. Two of them, Environmental Studies and History, Geography and Social Science, are directed at the primary and junior secondary age ranges and emphasise the relationship between history and other social studies subjects. Another, History 13–16, is an uncompromising single-subject project and is designed to lead pupils on to a new style G.C.E. or C.S.E. examination. In all three projects, history is not seen as a body of knowledge which must be learned, but as a method of analysing the past through the application of particular skills and concepts. This approach can be seen as a reflection of Bruner's assertion that for children of all age groups 'there is an appropriate version of any skill or knowledge' (Bruner 1968), a philosophy which has already transformed the teaching of science and mathematics. These projects might do the same for history and it is the intention of this chapter to examine them more closely and to consider some of their main implications.

Environmental Studies 5–13

The Environmental Studies Project 'was established to help teachers use the environment systematically to provide experiences that help the progressive development of a child's skills and concepts throughout his primary career and beyond' (Schools Council 1975). The skills are classified into (1) basic skills (particularly language and mathematical skills), (2) study skills, and (3) social skills, such as the exercise of responsibility and initiative. The study skills relevant to history include collecting and classifying all types of physical and social data (e.g. house types, architectural features, occupational structure – from census returns), mapping (e.g. activities based on nineteenth-century O.S. and tithe maps), interpreting photographs and sketches, and the preparation and presentation of interviews and questionnaires (e.g. as in oral history). Through the exercise of these skills, children will develop the general concepts of class, change and location, essential to an understanding of their environment.

The published guides for teachers include a general introduction which explains the thinking behind the project and demonstrates the potential interest of a wide variety of school environments, a very useful collection of accounts of the project in action, and two excellent method books covering some of the study skills (*Starting from Maps* and *Starting from Rocks*). It is disappointing that so little guidance is given on approaches through history, as the subject obviously has a major role in environmental studies (*Environmental Studies 5–13: The Use of Historical Resources* (Schools Council 1973) and *Study of a Village*, a kit of slides, charts and tapes available from Hart-Davis Educational, St Albans, go a little way towards meeting this deficiency).

As the environment of every school will present its own challenge and potential, there are no published materials for class use. Every school is free to interpret the guidelines in its own way although the need for closely coordinated planning among teachers in the same area is strongly emphasised. It would be unfortunate if local features were used too intensively and if teachers did not seek agreement on certain basic approaches to the fundamental study skills and concepts. There is an obvious need also to prevent the children becoming too insular in their view of the environment; to counterbalance any such tendency the historian, for example, could frequently move outwards into more general examinations of themes arising out of nineteenth-century industrial and social change.

History, Geography and Social Science 8–13

The History, Geography and Social Science 8–13 Project grew out

of a need to co-ordinate development work in history, geography and the social sciences in the middle years (of schooling). The aim of the Project is to formulate teaching objectives, with particular reference to progression in learning and styles of teaching, and to develop materials drawing on the three subject areas to be used by teachers whether in an integrated framework or otherwise. (Schools Council 1975)

From the beginning, the project team has involved practising teachers in the various planning stages, starting with a conference (1972) at which objectives and key concepts were discussed. The result of this collaboration was an extensive set of objectives embracing skills to be mastered, and attitudes, values and interests to be fostered, derived, of course, from the contributing areas of study. The skills have been subdivided into three sections: (a) intellectual skills, similar to the study skills of the Environmental Studies Project; (b) social skills, involving the ability to participate in social relationships within small groups and the ability to exercise empathy; (c) physical skills, relating mainly to manipulative and expressive skills. The project also suggests criteria that might be used to indicate, over a period of time, changes in children's attitudes, values and interests.

Content is not specified, but it is envisaged that the list of key concepts derived from social studies will influence both its selection and treatment. American curriculum developers have, for some time, attempted to compile such lists (*Man, A Course of Study* is a good example of a course constructed in this way). The 8–13 Project has opted for a relatively short list – Communication; Power; Values and Beliefs; Conflict/Consensus; Continuity/Change; Similarity/Difference; and Causality. Any such list must be an arbitrary one and the project is keen to see teachers drawing up their own. Topics will often be chosen with particular concepts in view, e.g. the Arab–Israeli conflict to develop understanding of the concepts of Power and Conflict. Or perhaps a popular topic such as the First World War might be studied within the context of Values and Beliefs as well as the more obvious ones of Power, Causality or Conflict. The project is well aware that the use of key concepts could result in a more controversial treatment of themes to the possible discomfort, perhaps, of the historian who has often regarded the development of attitudes and values as conflicting with objectivity.

The extent to which the project encourages the separate development of the social studies subjects is obviously a question of great concern to the history specialist. The project views each subject as a resource, as being valuable for its distinctive skills, content and approach, but suggests that it should be complemented by others during the middle years of schooling. This approach is in line with general trends in the academic world where there are signs that history is emerging from its isolationist phase and moving towards the social sciences. If we take an earlier example of content – the Arab–Israeli conflict – geography and economics in conjunction with history would certainly clarify the issues in a way that history alone could not. A family history project could also benefit enormously from sociological and economic contributions. History, then, is not threatened, but it is seen as having potentially valuable relationships with other social sciences. As the project puts it, interrelationship rather than integration is the term it would prefer to describe any association between the disciplines.

Another very relevant question concerns the translation into teaching/learning activities of the rationale behind the project. The project is at present engaged in an extensive publishing programme which will give a more comprehensive answer to this question than is possible here. It is clear, however, that the team has refused to be restricted by too narrow an interpretation of Piaget's stages of learning. For example, children must be encouraged to test hypotheses and generalisation, at first in very specific instances, but progressing gradually to more abstract examples. (The key concepts will obviously encourage this approach to learning.) Hypothesis testing will be familiar to the practising historian and one of the published units,

Clues, Clues, Clues, is an enterprising and interesting attempt to introduce children to this historian's use of evidence. What the contents of a dustbin have to tell us about the householder leads on to an examination of archaeological, visual and written evidence, culminating in a well-worked-out series of exercises on census returns. (Incidentally, the pack comes complete with master stencils for multiple production of teaching materials, a realistic attempt to avoid copyright infringements!)

The project emphasises the importance of developing empathy. For the historian, detailed study, as with the 'patch approach', is most likely to lead to a better appreciation and understanding of the behaviour of others. Games and simulation exercises, which can also be used to this end, feature prominently in the suggested learning activities. In one such exercise, the focal point is a proposed railway line between two towns. After research on likely problems and procedures, a role play exercise is staged in the form of a public inquiry into the project with children assuming the identities of the various interested parties. Obviously such an activity would take considerably longer than the usual allocation of time to nineteenth-century railway developments but to compensate for this there is a better chance of the class's involvement and interest in the topic.

Although the Environmental Studies Project and the History, Geography and Social Science Project have much to offer history in schools, their widespread adoption will not be easy. In the first place, teaching in this area of the curriculum in primary schools has generally been done, if done at all, in a haphazard, unstructured fashion. The topic or project – which encompasses social studies all too frequently – consists of laborious copying from barely understood reference books. Both projects challenge teachers to take the same care with history and associated subjects as they are accustomed to giving to mathematics and language skills. They call for carefully planned curricula in primary schools and for cooperation between primary and secondary schools. It might be argued also that they indicate a need for the provision in schools of specialists in these subjects, not to be responsible for all relevant teaching, but to be a source of inspiration and ideas. It is not enough for a teacher to familiarise himself with the facts about the Romans or the Vikings; he will need an insight into the methodology of the historian or the geographer, a demanding task for a non-specialist.

In the secondary school, other complications will arise. Teachers will need to be convinced that children do not have to embark on the relentless chronological progression to the chosen O level course at this stage. Historians, too, might need to be convinced that to interrelate their subject with other social studies and humanities subjects is not necessarily to endanger or dilute it. Timetabling needs to be more flexible also to accommodate fieldwork and the more time-consuming classroom activities such as games and simulation exercises.

More importantly, history teachers will need to give much greater consideration to the formulation of objectives and their translation into classroom activities. It is relatively simple to plan a term's work if the main objective is to provide an insight into a period of history. It is much more difficult if one is trying to develop a particular range of skills and attitudes. To plan work so that the inquiry process can operate with consequent posing of questions, forming of hypotheses, testing these hypotheses and arriving at a conclusion, is a daunting proposition.

History 13–16

If the two projects considered so far can be alleged to blur the distinctiveness of history, the same cannot be said of History 13–16. Despite any criticism one might have of this isolationist approach to history, it does fit in with the conventional school curriculum and any rethinking or reorganisation can be confined to one department. The project offers little that is new but it does embody the most widely accepted current notions about the teaching of history. For example, the first stage is designed to introduce thirteen- to fourteen-year-olds to the nature of history and the skills necessary for its study – the approach is very similar to that adopted by the History, Geography and Social Science Project with a detective exercise involving an examination of clues found on the body of a road accident casualty, leading ultimately to an archaeological exercise based on Sutton Hoo. This is followed by a presentation of the variety of evidence available for different periods of history (including Britain in the 1960s) and a rigorous examination of the problems associated with the evidence on the case of Richard III and the missing princes, and the Suffragette Derby of 1913. Finally, pupils are introduced to the kinds of questions historians ask about causation and motivation.

After the first stage, pupils embark on a second-year course leading to G.C.E. or C.S.E. This course includes a study in Development (Medicine), an Inquiry in Depth (e.g. Elizabethan England or the American West), Studies in Modern World History (e.g. The Rise of Communist China, The Irish Question), and History Around Us where visible evidence provides the starting point (e.g. Roman Britain, Industrial Archaeology). The course thus makes a welcome break from the chronological syllabus and offers something to the advocate of both contemporary world history and local history.

The first external examination of pupils takes place under the auspices of the Southern Universities Joint Board in the summer of 1976. This event will offer a real indication of the extent to which the project has been able to build on the approach to history embodied in the introductory unit. The existing traditional G.C.E. O level format with its emphasis firmly on essay writing and factual recall would not be relevant to a course that seeks to develop the skills of the historian. Indeed, the project will have made a real advance if it can draw up realistic criteria for assessing levels of achievement in a range of skills and develop an examination format that will adequately test them.

Conclusion

There is much common ground between the various projects relevant to history. It is particularly encouraging that all operate from the standpoint that 'to instruct someone in [a discipline] is not a matter of getting him to commit results to mind. Rather, it is to teach him to participate in the process that makes possible the establishment of knowledge' (Bruner 1968). Materials in the form of archive units and sets of documents are abundant, but hitherto a rationale and strategies for their use have been lacking. (Teachers might still feel that the History 13–16 Project might have been more forthcoming in this respect.)

It is unfortunate, however, that there is little evidence of close collaboration between the various projects. The History, Geography and Social Science team is aware of this problem:

Each project has gone its own way, with cordial but not close relationships with others, and then has emptied its ideas on the schools. This means that particular schools, and especially primary schools, have had to take on board one project after another, each making inadvertently large demands on time, effort and money. Little has really been done to see how they can fit harmoniously, or even at all, into the schools programme. (Blyth 1973)

Will primary and middle schools embrace the Environmental/Social Studies projects with real enthusiasm if the foundations they are laying are ignored in the secondary schools? Will children participate with interest and understanding if confronted with repetitive content and contradictory approaches? One would hope that the Schools Council might, as a next step, suggest possible ways of interlocking associated projects and thus lead the way to a more coherent presentation of the humanities and social studies curriculum than we now have. Certainly for the primary and middle years of schooling, approaches and materials from the Environmental Studies and the History, Geography and Social Science Projects could be very effectively used in conjunction with each other. The latter, also, could serve as a good foundation for History 13–16. It is too easy to imply that teachers themselves must construct their own syllabuses from the options available to them. Many do not have the time or the enterprise to do this, and it is surely the responsibility of the Schools Council to ensure that the efforts of its project teams are made as accessible as possible to the average as well as to the committed teacher. At the same time, authorities have a responsibility to encourage teachers to acquaint themselves with these developments and to provide the resources necessary for their adoption.

Schools Council projects: relevant publications

ENVIRONMENTAL STUDIES 5–13
Publisher: Hart-Davis
  Teacher's Guide (1972)
  Case Studies (1972)
  Starting from Maps (1972)
  Starting from Rocks (1972)
Schools Council, *Environmental Studies 5–13: The Use of Historical Sources*, working paper 48 (London, 1973: Evans/Methuen)
R. W. Crossland and S. D. F. Moore, *Environmental Studies Project (5–13): An Evaluation* (London, 1974: Macmillan)

HISTORY, GEOGRAPHY AND SOCIAL SCIENCE 8–13
Publisher: Collins Educational and E.S.L.
Teachers' publications:
  Place, Time and Society 8–13: An Introduction (1975)
  Curriculum Planning in History, Geography and Social Science 8–13 (1975)
  Games and Simulations in the Classroom (1975)
  Teaching for Concepts (1975)
  Evaluation, Assessment and Record Keeping (1975)
  To be published 1976/7:
  Using Social Statistics
  Using Sources and Resources
  Teaching for Empathy
  Teaching Critical Thinking Skills
  Themes in Outline
Pupils' Units (multi-media) of interest to the historian include:
  (a) *Shops*
  (b) *Clues*
  (c) *Life in the 1930s*
Units to be published 1976/7:
  (a) *Victorians*
  (b) *People and Machines*

(c) *Village and Town*
(d) *People and Progress*

HISTORY 13–16
Materials to be published by Holmes McDougal
> A newsletter and a 16 mm film, *A New Look at History*, are available from the History 13–16 Project, Institute of Education, The University, Leeds.

PART III

13 The training of the history teacher: the key to the future?

The reader must have been struck by the apparent contradiction between the general criticism of history teaching – typified by the recent comment of Harries (1975) that 'There is concern that history in school is often purposeless, taught by chalk, talk and textbook as thin and useless information' – and the evidence contained in the first two parts of this book which indicates that a great deal is happening and that history teaching is in a far from moribund state. The two views can, however, be reconciled. History – at least some aspect of it – is taught in nearly all primary or secondary schools, but the influence of the reforming movement, active though it is, has touched only a minority of these. Thus, although it may be desirable to get more pedagogical coherence, for example in developing the more structured theory of history teaching hinted at in Chapter 12, the immediate priority for the future is to ensure that the knowledge we already possess is applied on a much wider scale. The way forward must lie in the improved education of the history teacher, at both initial and in-service levels. The general idea is by no means new – in 1895 the Bryce Commission commented that it was 'above all, in the supply of more highly educated and skilful teachers, that educational progress must in future consist'. Ultimately history in the classroom depends on the qualities, skills and knowledge of the individual teacher, so the character of his education is a matter of crucial importance.

Research on the training of teachers of history in the nineteenth century (Steele 1974) has suggested that it is not so much the content of what students learn as the way in which they learn it that determines the methods they will adopt in the classroom. In 1837, for example, students at Borough Road were asked in their examination on the art of teaching to consider the extent to which the general principles adopted by Pestalozzi could be carried out in teaching history (Dunn 1837). Yet they were taught by lectures and expressed their ideas in essays and such methods were more characteristic of nineteenth-century school history teaching than those advocated by Pestalozzi! Forty years later, in fact, students at Borough Road were still encountering history in the traditional manner. A student at this college (Ballard 1937) recollected vividly the approach to history of J. C. Curtis who taught at Borough Road for over twenty years and who was held up as an example to all by no less a figure than Matthew Arnold:

It was not dictation, nor exposition, but inquisition. It consisted in asking questions – and nothing else – not in the manner of Socrates, but in the manner of Thomas Gradgrind. In this subject he had published two books; a *Date Book* which was small and innocent, and a *School and College History of England*, which was a work of monumental dullness. The *Date Book*, innocuous enough in itself, became in his hand a weapon of offence. For we had to learn it off by heart, word for word. And nothing would do but *ipsissima verba*. If a student said that in '55 B.C. a Roman General called Julius Caesar invaded Britain', when the textbook said that in '55 B.C. Julius Caesar, a Roman General, invaded Britain', he was accounted wrong and was reprimanded for not having prepared his lesson.

School history was characterised by a heavy emphasis on the accurate regurgitation of factual information and it is not difficult to see why!

In the present period there is a need to clarify thinking about the way in which teachers are educated. Consideration must be given to the ways in which students approach both history and the teaching of history. There are obvious differences between the nature and content of the two, but the gap between them is not as wide as it might at first appear. It is the way in which the student approaches both history and the teaching of history which will affect his attitudes and skills, and this in turn will eventually be reflected in the classroom situation.

The historical education of the teacher

The variety of experiences encountered by history students in universities and colleges has already been touched on in Chapter 2. The experience of the writer, encountering successive history postgraduate students embarking on an education course, is that they tend to see history in a very blinkered way. Frequently they judge themselves as historians by what they can remember of the past and tend to assume that, through possession of that knowledge, they have acquired a greater understanding of the society in which they live – a respect for their cultural heritage, an insight into the future and an ability to be critical and objective and to make informed decisions – and that in some mysterious way they will communicate these to the pupils they teach. The reality is usually quite different. Their understanding of the nature of different types of evidence is reasonable, but their ability to use it is restricted, and they tend to be almost totally deficient in fieldwork skills. Invariably they are at their most uncomfortable when asked to work in a group on a historical project. Thus it is not enough that students understand the nature of the subject and that they are able to write, at a theoretical level, about how it may be approached. It must become second nature to them to formulate their own hypotheses, exercise skills of analysis on evidence they have found for themselves, express their own conclusions and work in conjunction with others. Only if it becomes habitual for the student to think and work in this way will he seek to encourage the same qualities in the children he teaches.

There is evidence that university and college courses are moving in this direction. Beckwith (1971) has argued that considerable use is being made of local and other sources. Certainly there are enterprising schemes in existence. Johnson (1971) has suggested the use of a questionnaire by groups of students to analyse particular types of documents. Each of a group of students, for example, might analyse fifty probate inventories on the basis of an agreed questionnaire, so gaining an individual understanding of that particular type of evidence while at the same time collectively producing a mass of information which could well form the basis of some original and worthwhile research. Such an approach would have the advantages of encouraging students to work together while at the same time motivating them more highly as they would be producing more original material. At the same time, through experience, they would be acquiring an understanding of history quite different from that they would have been likely to acquire in a lecture on probate inventories (or on other sources – parish records, poor law records, quarter sessions records, etc. – that might be approached in a similar way).

Similarly Thompson and Gabert (1975) found a meaningful way of introducing students at Chorley College to history. During the first term planned tasks, approached in small groups, replaced lectures. A separate local topic was taken each week and approached through a variety of sources. Thus the study of the theme 'urban growth' involved using geological and O.S. maps and plans, directories, the Chorley Public Health Report of 1853, and engaging in fieldwork in Chorley. In each session students were encouraged to assess their sources and were advised on methods of recording and presenting ideas and information. Clearly there are limitations to such an approach but Thompson and Gabert found it very good for discussion and developing working relationships while, as they noted: 'The historian's sources were no longer a mystery; respect for his work and problems increased; the study of history had become more meaningful, real and enjoyable.' The first priority at this level is the provision of a good historical education, yet it must be apparent that such a training could have, indirectly, a very beneficial effect or history in the classroom.

Another aspect of the student's historical education which tends to be greatly neglected is his familiarisation with the repositories of sources such as museums and record offices. It is only through their regular use that the student acquires the knowledge, skill and confidence to use them as a matter of course. Thus history students at Madeley College are introduced to the Staffordshire County Record

Office at an early stage in their course and, in producing local studies, they are encouraged to make extensive use of such repositories, partly in anticipation of their using them when they have left college. In this context it was found, for example, that 30–40 per cent of students at Summerfield College, Kidderminster, who were introduced to the local museum subsequently made use of its services, and this in turn proved a spur to teachers in schools (Vodden and Blench 1971).

One of the basic factors restricting innovation in schools is the teacher's unwillingness to concede that he is 'uncertain' about what he does. He identifies strongly with the knowledge and skills he already possesses and because, in innovating, he is likely to be asked to acquire new skills, he must acknowledge incompetence in these areas. As such an acknowledgement does not come easily, the pace of change is slow. Many history students leave university or college lacking in basic historical skills; one important and obvious way to improve the teaching of history in the future would be to provide a more complete and meaningful historical education.

Training in the teaching of history

INITIAL TRAINING

It is evident that the initial training of history teachers is in a far from satisfactory condition. The pilot scheme for the induction of new teachers in Liverpool investigated the attitude of those teachers towards their preparation in initial training courses for school history teaching. Only 14 per cent thought they were starting out with some 'solid, practical relevant preparation' while the remainder, considering their training in relation to their experience in schools, concluded that it had been 'unstructured, related to only one type of school (usually the Grammar School), theoretical rather than practical in character, limited to a few tips during teaching practice, or non-existent' (Davies and Pritchard 1975). Comments typical of student attitudes towards their training in history teaching were recorded by Fogg (1974) – 'Our lecturers placed great emphasis on keeping rigidly to planned lessons, writing out every question we would ask and anticipating every answer. Whereas in reality the most important skill is to be continually flexible within the general pattern', and a mournful 'When I think of the time that we spent planning imaginary lessons, for imaginary classes of idealised pupils . . .' If history is to be taught more effectively in the future we must question the assumptions on which the present pattern of initial training is based.

Two major areas of interest stand out in initial training – the theoretical approach to the teaching of history, which is usually college-based, and the practical work, which is undertaken in schools. Courses devised in the former tend to be logical in their construction, but frequently take little account of student psychology. There tends to be concentration on what the student should know and be able to do, rather than on how he can best acquire the knowledge and skills thought desirable. Sylvester (1975) argues that the student should know what history is, and the various ways in which history may be approached. He states that the student should also consider the purpose and value of teaching history in school and further argues that lesson-planning activities, the practice of classroom techniques and the production of materials should play an important part in professional studies. The logic of what Sylvester advises is unquestionable, but such points have been made for over a century without securing the desired effect. The statement of what history teachers should know and be able to do will not in itself improve the training of history teachers and subsequently the teaching of history in the classroom.

A systematic attempt to devise a coherent set of objectives for the professional preparation of teachers in history and social studies – in this case in primary schools – has been made by Gunning and Gunning (1974). This has involved the grouping of objectives on such themes as 'motivation' and 'evaluation'. The theme 'amendment of plans', for example, states:

Students would be asked to assume that some activity has failed (children not learning: noise and confusion). They would then advance hypotheses as to the cause of failure. They would mention (i) lack of motivation, (ii) excessive difficulty of material, (iii) excessive easiness of material, (iv) lack of clarity in setting tasks. They would be asked to assume that one of these hypotheses is substantially correct and asked how they would alter the next activity. They would then (i) re-order the plan for the next activity on that theme appropriately, (ii) re-order the plan for subsequent activities appropriately.

It must be emphasised that the Gunnings did not see their objectives being achieved through lecture and discussion. Skills, for example, were to be acquired through practice – either individually or in groups. Even so the artificial nature of the objective stated is evident and it is unlikely that the student would find the associated activities as meaningful as might be intended.

Assumptions about the value of teaching practice must also be called into question. Lewis (1975) has noted that, as a learning experience for the student, teaching practice does not even meet a rudimentary set of objectives. Students tend to see it as teaching rather than practice. They concern themselves with satisfying the supervisor or class teacher and with assessment. Take for instance the case of the unfortunate student who 'geared one of his lessons to suit a particular Tutor's enthusiasms, [when] a different tutor came in instead and slated the technique used. A similar lesson was then given to the "right" tutor and enthusiastically received' (Fogg 1974). It is not surprising that students do play safe, as assessment is very important in their eyes. Thus, if progress is to be made, the whole context of the students' learning must be changed and the problems of teaching children must become the prime focus of interest (Lewis 1975).

The classroom experience must become much more of a cooperative venture with the emphasis on the professional character of the work involved. Student, teacher and supervisor have to work together on the problems of teaching history to children, the student being fortified by the experience and theoretical insight of the other two, while the ideas and suggestions of the latter can be put to a practical test. Similarly, the syllabuses suggested by theorists such as Sylvester and the Gunnings might well be used as a framework to provide a coherent basis for the student's work within the classroom.

An initial training based on these ideas demands radical rethinking on the part of those responsible for the professional preparation of teachers. They must recognise the need to separate the learning experience of the student and his assessment. The class teacher will have to widen his professional perspective to take account of his extended role, and the supervisor must be released for a greater proportion of time so that he can make a more effective contribution to work in the classroom.

Progress is being made towards a more professional training for history teachers. One of the most enterprising schemes for providing the student with a more extended experience in school, and which involves the teacher more fully in the student's preparation, is the postgraduate course at Sussex University. Initiated in 1965, this is essentially school-based, the student spending three days a week in school and two in the university. Within the school students are supervised by a practising teacher, but both students and teacher maintain a close link with the university (Lamont 1972). The benefits of the extended period in schools are reflected, for example, in the work of Bysshe and Gould (1975) who, during their year (1973–4) as postgraduate students at Sussex, produced two games – 'Aggression' and 'The Coketown Election Game' while on teaching practice at Christ's Hospital. Such an activity demands the coordination of theory and practice in relation to a specific situation and, as such, obviously provides the students with a more meaningful and professionally stimulating experience. The key to success is the way in which the student is learning rather than the content of what he learns and the effects of the experience are likely to be much more enduring than would be the case in a traditional pattern of teaching practice.

IN-SERVICE TRAINING

The most problematic area, but that which probably has the greatest potential for the future of history teaching, is in-service training. It is possible for the serving teacher to develop his teaching skills through attending specialist courses or, if he has the will to do so, to improve himself through his own efforts. Both approaches are likely to increase in importance in the next few years and they merit detailed consideration.

Organisers of in-service courses face many practical difficulties. Wenham (1974) surveyed in-service work in teachers' centres and found that, although there had been significant progress towards professional development in some, the lack of day-release schemes had proved a major barrier. In addition he noted how replies from some centres indicated that 'lack of interest, unwillingness to give up time outside of school hours, and devotion to the status quo on the part of some teachers' had also proved serious obstacles. The reluctance of teachers to embark on courses is not hard to understand. The pressures within school are considerable while, at first glance, many of the courses seem less relevant to the teachers' needs in that they appear geared to a theoretical approach to history teaching, whereas the teachers invariably look for practical help and guidance. The irony is that it is impossible to separate theory from practice and courses that appear practical inevitably focus attention on the theoretical issues involved. Even so it is what a teacher understands a course to offer that is important in securing his commitment to it.

A good example of an in-service course which was successful and which attracted support partly because of its practical implications was held at Eastbourne College (Bolwell and Lines 1972). Recognising the teachers' lack of confidence in using the facilities of museums, county archive offices, etc., Bolwell and Lines set up an in-service workshop in which the teachers built up resource kits to use with their own classes. The teachers were advised by the tutors on the collection of materials and their use, and it is inconceivable that in so doing the basic curriculum question of 'what', 'how' and 'why' would not be raised. Similarly a course on teaching environmental studies in the first school at Madeley College in 1975 was deliberately geared to a practical approach. Teachers worked, for example, in a graveyard making rubbings of gravestones, and compiling statistics for graph work based on the popularity of Christian names in different periods, and on mortality rates, etc. Subsequent discussions raised fundamental theoretical questions about the appropriateness of particular types of material and techniques in the classroom. In addition the teachers had acquired new skills through practice and they proved much more willing to try out their ideas with children. Indeed it was found that in the example quoted above they developed their own ideas. The use of creative writing, based on activities in the graveyard, produced excellent results in a class of seven-year-olds. The examples are simple but nevertheless significant in that they illustrate that the teacher will come more readily to theory through considering practice, and that it is the way in which the teacher works that is important in producing change within the classroom.

A college that stands out in the promotion of in-service education for history teachers is C. F. Mott College of Education in Liverpool. There, considerable efforts have been made to promote the academic respectability of professional work and to marry happily the theoretical and practical elements involved. In 1975–6, for example, the college ran a course leading to a Diploma in Historical Education, an integral part of which was the conducting of a research project within the schools of course members (Davies and Pritchard 1975). Such a requirement is calculated to develop the professional expertise of the course member. In addition the award of a diploma serves to emphasise the academic respectability of such work and it has the added advantage of attracting teachers anxious to improve their qualifications.

Unfortunately in-service courses touch only a minority of history teachers and there seems little prospect in the immediate future that economic conditions will allow any substantial expansion in their provision. There is therefore serious cause for concern because, as Harries (1975) concluded after conducting an inquiry into the conceptions of history teaching and in-service training in history of 120 London teachers of children in the nine to thirteen age range, 'in general teachers need more effective training in the teaching of history than they are at present given. Many appear to have only a limited understanding of its nature and the purposes of its study. This must affect the value of their work.' A widespread improvement in history teaching can only be achieved in the foreseeable future if many more history teachers than those who will be involved in in-service courses can be persuaded of the need to improve themselves. They must acquire the qualities of what Stenhouse (1975) has termed the 'extended professional', i.e. a capacity for autonomous self-development through systematic self-study and through the study of the work of other teachers, and by testing out ideas in classroom research procedures. The basic problem is to find ways of persuading the individual teacher that there is a need for him to become more professional in his outlook. Somehow he must be brought to recognise the uniqueness of his own classroom situation and that a professional approach to teaching requires that he see his classroom as the place in which he is the researching agent − formulating his own hypotheses and testing and adapting his ideas. It might seem at first glance that an idealised picture of the professional teacher is being built up which is beyond the capacity of the ordinary teacher to achieve. Fortunately this need not be the case: evidence exists which suggests that the teacher has the capacity and means to improve himself if he has the will to do so.

In this context the work of the Ford Teaching Project (1975) is of particular interest. Based on the Centre for Applied Research in the University of East Anglia the project explored the idea of inquiry/discovery teaching and worked on the basis that the forty teachers involved should contribute to the development of theory about classroom practice, as well as playing a full part in the practical aspects of the project. Teacher members of the project explored various techniques for self-evaluation. The tape recorder was used in a variety of ways. It was employed for instance to analyse teachers' questioning techniques, children's questions, both teachers' and children's vocabulary, and children's level of comprehension, as well as for recording the opinions and criticisms of pupils and others. The reaction of one teacher to a playback of a class discussion in which she looked at her own role in that discussion is interesting:

I had no idea how much discussion was dominated by me, how rarely I allowed children to finish their comments, what leading questions I asked, how much I gave away what I considered to be 'right' answers. This experience resulted in my completely rethinking my teaching approach (which I'd always believed was very child-centred) and I taped a series of discussions to record and monitor my own progress.

The tape recorder could obviously be a useful instrument for the history teacher anxious to improve his teaching. It is an aid available in most schools; its use need not interfere with the normal course of the lesson, and it need not occupy too much time in follow-up work, since the taping of just a small part of a single lesson might produce useful material. It would be essential, however, for the history teacher to be clear about what he wanted to find out before he started, but the possibilities are endless. A lesson on the Norman Conquest, for example, might have one of a number of objectives. The teacher might be trying to develop interest in the subject; provide a narrative of the main events; develop a sense of drama; promote discussion of the issues involved – moral, military, etc. – test the children's understanding of the historical vocabulary involved, or his own use of that vocabulary; or pinpoint the difficulties encountered by a group working on a project associated with the Conquest. The analysis of a tape in which the teacher was clear about his objectives might well throw up some interesting results and so lead to the stimulation of a more professional approach to history teaching.

The use of the tape recorder was just one of the techniques employed by members of the Ford Teaching Project. Others included the multiple interview (including the use of an outside observer), interviewing pupils, the questionnaire and the making of field notes. Clearly such techniques could be used by teachers of any subject, but that does not invalidate their use by the history teacher. It may well be optimistic to hope that the mass of history teachers who have remained largely untouched by developments in history teaching in recent years will suddenly be seized with a desire to improve themselves and engage in frantic programmes of self-education. On the other hand, the general criticism of history teaching is such that more widespread reform is urgently required and, as the teacher is the ultimate agent determining what actually happens in the classroom, the means have to be found to persuade him to become more professional in outlook.

Conclusion

Freeman (1879) commented 'It is because history is so untechnical a subject, a subject so open to all, a subject seemingly so easy, a subject on which everybody can talk and write and form an opinion, that the way in which it is commonly taught is so unsufferably bad.' The same explanation might well be offered for the poor standards achieved in history teaching in many classrooms today. The teaching of history is in fact a skilled and complex process which demands a highly professional approach. The evidence contained in this book points to the fact that great progress is being made in a variety of areas, in particular the development of children's thinking in history, the formulation of aims and objectives, the setting of examinations, and the evolution of new teaching strategies – the source method, drama, games and simulations, etc. The contributions of the teachers indicate that, at a grassroots level, individual teachers are striving to make the study of history a more meaningful and worthwhile experience for children. The activities of the Schools Council project teams reflect the concern of teachers and academics that the teaching of history should be seen in a professional light. Enough is already known about enlightened approaches to the teaching of history, which, if applied on a wide scale, could radically alter the image of the subject in children's eyes. The key to the future lies therefore in persuading those teachers who fit into the mould described by Freeman that there is a need to become more professional in their approach, and that the means exist to enable them to do so. It is hoped that this final chapter goes some way towards suggesting solutions to this basic problem.

References *and* Name index

BALDWIN, E. (1807) *History of England*. London, Hodgkins. *1*

BALLARD, P. B. (1937) *Things I Cannot Forget*. London, University of London Press. *106*

BARKER, B. (1974) Fresh approach to history. *T.E.S.*, No 3075, 20. *2*

BATE, P., and MOORE, E. (1975) Learning historical thinking does make a difference. *Teaching History*, 4 No 13, 9–12. *16*

BATHO, G. R. (1972) The crisis of the source method. *T.E.S.*, No 2966, 51. *56*

BECKWITH, I. (1971) Archives and local history in teacher education – some second thoughts. *Education for Teaching*, 86, 48–51. *107*

BEEVERS, R. (1969) History and social science. *Trends in Education*, 14, 9–13. *13*

BERNBAUM, G. (1972) Language and history teaching. In Burston and Green (1972), 39–50. *17, 21*

BLISHEN, E. (1969) *The School That I'd Like*. London, Penguin. *4*

BLOOM, B. S., and KRATHWOHL, D. R. (1956) *Taxonomy of Educational Objectives*: Handbook 1, *The Cognitive Domain*. New York, McKay. *32*

BLOWS, R. P. (1971) *History at the Universities*. London, Historical Association. *8, 10*

BLYTH, W. A. L. (1973) *Spotlights: A Summary of the Project's Approach*. Liverpool, Schools Council. *101*

BOLWELL, L. H., and LINES, C. J. (1972) Resources for local studies in primary and middle schools: an in-service experiment. *Teaching History*, 2 No 8, 320–6. *113*

BRADLEY, N. (1947) The growth of knowledge of time in children of school age. *British Journal of Psychology*, 38, 67–78. Quoted in Jahoda (1963). *19*

BRAMWELL, R. D. (1973) Curricular determinants: an historical perspective. *History of Education Society Bulletin*, 12, 40–9. *7*

BRUNER, J. S. (1960) *The Process of Education*. New York, Vintage. *23*

BRUNER, J. S. (1968) *Towards a Theory of Instruction*. New York, Norton. *55, 94, 101*

BRYANT, M. (1972) No 'wild rush to the present in five instalments'. *T.E.S.*, No 2966, 47. *3*

BUCKNALL, J. (1974) History and examinations. *Teaching History*, 3 No 12, 360–3. *38, 55*

BURRELL, D. (1972) Emphasis on the New Europe. *T.E.S.*, No 2966, 48. *50*

BURSTON, W. H., and GREEN, M. A. (1972) (eds) *Handbook for History Teachers*. London, Methuen.

BUSH, M. L. (1973) Outlines versus themes. *History*, 58 No 94, 384–91. *10*

BYSSHE, S., and GOULD, C. (1975) The use of games in the teaching of history. *Teaching History*, 4 No 14, 132–7. *112*

CAMBRIDGE INSTITUTE OF EDUCATION (1970) *The Teaching of History to the 11–14 Age Group*. Cambridge Institute of Education. *28, 45*

CHANAN, G. (1974) Objectives in the humanities. *Educational Research*, 16, 198–205. *30*

CHARLTON, K. (1952) The comprehension of historical terms. Unpublished B.Ed. thesis, University of Glasgow. *17*

COHEN, J., HANSEL, C. E. M., and SYLVESTER, J. (1954) An experimental study of comparative judgments of time. *British Journal of Psychology*, 45, 108–114. *25*

COLLISTER, P. (1972) History teaching today. *Trends in Education*, 27, 2–5. *4*

COLTHAM, J. B. (1960) Junior school children's understanding of historical terms. Unpublished Ph.D. thesis, University of Manchester. *17*

COLTHAM, J. B. (1971) *The Development of Thinking and the Learning of History*. London, Historical Association. *18, 20, 24, 25*

COLTHAM, J. B. (1972) Educational objectives and the teaching of history. *Teaching History*, 2 No 7, 278–9. *34*

COLTHAM, J. B., and FINES, J. (1971) *Educational Objectives for the Study of History*. London, Historical Association. *32*

CONNELL-SMITH, G., and LLOYD, H. (1974) *The Relevance of History*. London, Heinemann. *7*

COOK, T. D. (1970) Local history: some practical approaches. *Teaching History*, 1 No 3, 164–73. *53*

DANBY, T. W. (1880) Report on the schools of Ipswich and Edmonton. In *Report of the Committee of Council on Education 1880–1*. London, H.M.S.O. 267. *1*

DAVIES, B., and PRITCHARD, P. (1975) History still in danger. *Teaching History*, 4 No 14, 113–16. *109, 114*

DE SILVA, W. A. (1969) Concept formation in adolescence through contextual cues, with special reference to historical material. Unpublished Ph.D. thesis University of Birmingham. Quoted in Honeybone (1971). *23*

DE SILVA, W. A. (1972) The formation of historical concepts through contextual cues. *Educational Review*, 24, 174–82. *16*

DOCKING, J. W. (1970) History and the C.S.E. *Teaching History*, 1 No 4, 292–6. *38*

DOUCH, R. (1970) Local history. In M. Ballard (ed.), *New Movements in the Study and Teaching of History*. London, Temple Smith, 105–15. *52*

DUNN, H. (1837) *Popular Education*. London, The Sunday-School Union. *106*

ELTON, G. R. (1967) *The Practice of History*. London, Methuen. *4*

FINES, J. (1969) (ed.) *History*. London, Blond. *2*

FINES, J., and VERRIER, R. L. (1974) *The Drama of History: An Experiment in Co-operative Teaching*. London, New University Education. *60*

FIRTH, C. H. (1904) *A Plea for the Historical Teaching of History*. Oxford, Clarendon Press. *8*

FLICKINGER, A., and REHAGE, K. J. (1949) Building time and space concepts. In National Council for the Social Studies, *20th Yearbook*. Quoted in Jahoda (1963). *19*

FOGG, E. (1974) Training history teachers: a school view. *History Teaching Review*, 6 No 1, 8–10. *109, 111*

FORD TEACHING PROJECT (1975) Unit 2 *Research Methods, Ways of Doing Research in One's Own Classroom*. Norwich, Centre for Advanced Research in Education. *115*

FREEMAN, E. A. (1879) *How the Study of History is Let and Hindered*. Liverpool. *2, 116*

GASSON, P. C., and STOKES, W. E. (1972) G.C.E. (ordinary level) and C.S.E. examinations. In Burston and Green (1972), 173–86. *41*

GILES, P. M. (1973) History in the secondary school: a survey. *Journal of Curriculum Studies*, 5/2, 133–45. *27*

GILES, P. M., and NEAL, G. (1973) History teaching analysed. *Trends in Education*, 32, 16–25. *34*

GOWLING, M. (1975) What's science to history or history to science? *T.H.E.S.*, No 194, 9. *8*

GUNNING, D., and GUNNING, S. (1974) Some considerations on professional studies courses in new B.Ed. degree with reference to history and social studies in the primary school. *Education for Teaching*, 95, 51–9. *110*

HALLAM, R. N. (1967) Logical thinking in history. *Educational Review*, 13, 183–202. *15*

HALLAM, R. N. (1970) Piaget and thinking in history. In M. Ballard (ed.), *New Movements in the Study and Teaching of History*. London, Temple Smith. *20, 22*

HANNAM, C. L. (1968) What's wrong with history? *New Era*, 49 No 8, 211–18. *17*

HARRIES, E. (1975) Teachers' conceptions of history teaching. *Teaching History*, 4 No 14, 151–3. *105, 114*

HARRISON, B. (1968) History at the universities 1968: a commentary. *History*, 53, 357–80. *9*

HEATER, D. B. (1968) The place of contemporary world history in the school curriculum. *Higher Education Journal*, 16, 10–12. *50*

HONEYBONE, M. (1971) The development of formal historical thought in schoolchildren. *Teaching History*, 2 No 16, 147–52. *23*

HOSKINS, W. G. (1967) *Fieldwork in Local History*. London, Faber. *52*

HURSTFIELD, J. (1968) The historian's commitment. *T.E.S.*, No 2762, 1383. *12*

HURSTFIELD, J. (1969) The undergraduate historian. In The Historical Association, *History in the Sixth Form and in Higher Education*. London, Historical Association. 4–8. *12*

JAHODA, G. (1963) Children's concepts of time and history. *Educational Review*, **16** No 1, 87–104. *18, 25*

JEFFREYS, M. V. C. (1939) *History in Schools: The Study of Development*. London, Pitman. *47*

JOHNSON, J. A. (1971) Group questionnaries and the teaching of local history in colleges of education. *Teaching History*, **2** No 6, 143–6. *107*

JONES, J. A. P. (1972) Maidstone G.S. Mode III history 'O' level. *Teaching History*, **2** No 7, 272–5. *42*

JONES, R. BEN (1973) (ed.) *Practical Approaches to the New History*. London, Hutchinson.

KRATHWOHL, D. R., BLOOM, B. S., and MASIA, B. B. (1964) *Taxonomy of Educational Objectives*: Handbook II, *The Affective Domain*. New York, McKay. *32*

LAMONT, W. (1972) (ed.) *The Realities of Teaching History*. Edinburgh, Sussex University Press. *112*

LATHAM, H. (1877) *On the Action of Examinations Considered as a Means of Selection*. Cambridge, Deighton-Bell. *36*

LEWIS, I. (1975) Teacher training: professional or peripheral? *Education for Teaching*, **96**, 35–42. *111*

LONGMAN GROUP (1973) History Games. York, Longman Group Ltd Resources Unit. *72*

LUTHY, H. (1968) What's the point of history? *Journal of Contemporary History*, **3**, 3–22. *11*

MACINTOSH, H. G. (1971) Assessment in 'O' level history. *Teaching History*, **2** No 5, 53–7. *41*

MEDLYCOTT, J. (1973) Drama and medieval history. *Teaching History*, **3** No 9, 26–8. *60*

MILBURN, J. (1972) Simulations in history teaching: promising innovation or passing fad? *Teaching History*, **2** No 7, 236–41. *58, 59*

MILNE, A. (1973) Project work at 'O' level: a review of a recent pilot scheme. In Jones (1973), 132–60. *42*

MILNE, A. T. (1974) History at the universities: then and now. *History*, **59** No 195, 33–46. *9*

MURPHY, B. J. (1971) History through the family. *Teaching History*, **2** No 5, 1–8. *58*

MUSGROVE, F. (1963) Five scales of attitude to history. *Studies in Education*, **3**, 423–39. *24*

OAKDEN, E. C., and STURT, M. (1922) The development of the knowledge of time in children. *British Journal of Psychology*, **12**, 309–36. Quoted in Jahoda (1963). *19*

PALMER, M. (1973) Using stimulus material. In Jones (1973), 84–108.   *34*

PAYNE, J. (1875) Discussion on the teaching of history. *Educational Times*, **27** No 166, 252.   *55*

PEEL, E. A. (1967) Some problems in the psychology of history teaching. In W. H. Burston and D. Thompson (eds), *Studies in the Nature and Teaching of History*. London, Routledge. 159–90.   *18*

PLOWDEN REPORT (1967) *Children and Their Primary Schools*. London, H.M.S.O.   *53*

PRESTON, G. (1969) The value of local history in the school curriculum. *Teaching History*, **1** No 2, 87–91.   *53*

PRIESTLEY, J. (1788) *Lectures on History and General Policy*. Birmingham, J. Johnson.   *8*

RAYNER, E. (1972) American history in schools. *Teaching History*, **2** No 7, 261–4.   *59*

ROBERTS, M. (1972) Educational objectives for the study of history. *Teaching History*, **2** No 8, 347–50.   *42*

ROGERS, J. (1967) History needs a revolution. *The Teacher*, **10** No 13, 14.   *5*

ROGERS, K. W. (1967) Concepts of time in secondary school children of above average I.Q. *British Journal of Educational Psychology*, **37**, 99–109.   *19*

ROOTS, D. E. (1970) An investigation into the use of fieldwork in history teaching. *Teaching History*, **1** No 4, 269–71.   *53*

RUSSELL, C. (1968) From school to university. *T.E.S.*, No 2762, 1385.   *12*

SCHOOLS COUNCIL (1968) Enquiry 1, *Young School Leavers*. London, H.M.S.O.   *3, 24*

SCHOOLS COUNCIL (1968) Examination Bulletin No 18, *The Certificate of Secondary Education: The Place of the Personal Topic – History*. London, H.M.S.O.   *39*

SCHOOLS COUNCIL (1969) *Humanities for the Young School Leaver: An Approach Through History*. London, Evans/Methuen.   *10*

SCHOOLS COUNCIL (1973) *Environmental Studies 5–13: The Use of Historical Sources*. Working paper 48. London, Evans/Methuen.   *95*

SCHOOLS COUNCIL (1975) *Curriculum Research and Developments in the Humanities and Social Studies*. London, Schools Council.   *96*

SMITH, B. O., STANLEY, W. O., and SHORES, J. H. (1971) Cultural roots of the curriculum. In R. Hooper (ed.), *The Curriculum: Context, Design and Development*. Edinburgh, Oliver and Boyd. 16–19.   *7*

STACEY, T. (1969) Teaching recent history backwards. *Teaching History*, **1** No 2, 107–8.   *48*

STEEL, D. J., and TAYLOR, L. (1973) *Family History in Schools*. London, Phillimore.   *57*

STEELE, I. J. D. (1974) A study of the formative years of the development of the history curriculum in English schools 1833–1901. Unpublished Ph.D. thesis, University of Sheffield.   *106*

STENHOUSE, L. (1975) *An Introduction to Curriculum Research and Development.* London, Heinemann. *41, 55, 115*

STONES, S. K. (1965) An analysis of the growth of adolescent thinking in relation to the complexities of school history material. Unpublished research of the University of Birmingham. *16*

SONES, S. K. (1967) Factors influencing the capacity of adolescents to think in abstract terms in the understanding of history. Unpublished M.Ed. thesis, University of Manchester. *21*

STROTZKA, H. (1971) The necessity of teaching world history. *The New Era*, **52**, 408–12. *50*

SYLVESTER, D. (1975) Professional studies and history. *Education for Teaching*, **97**, 55–8. *110*

THE OPEN UNIVERSITY (1970) *Humanities Foundation Course*, Unit 5 *What History Is and Why It is Important.* Milton Keynes, Open University Press. *27*

THOMPSON, G., and GABERT, H. (1975) An approach to the history course in a college of education. *Teaching History*, **4** No 14, 117–20. *108*

THORNTON, P. A. (1971) The play's the thing. *Teaching History*, **2** No 6, 125–30. *60*

TURNER, D. (1974) Population studies in the history syllabus. *Teaching History*, **3** No 12, 230–3. *57*

VODDEN, D. F., and BLENCH, B. J. R. (1971) Museum work in a college of education. *Teaching History*, **2** No 5, 15–20. *109*

WALLACE, J. G. (1965) *Concept Growth and the Education of the Child.* Slough, N.F.E.R. *19, 20*

WENHAM, P. (1974) History at teachers' centres. *Teaching History*, **3** No 11, 245–9. *113*

WOOD, R. G. E. (1973) Archive units for teaching. *Teaching History*, **3** No 9, 41–6. *56*

Subject index